Breaking the Nuclear Impasse

The Century Foundation is grateful to the Italian Ministry of Foreign Affairs for its generous support of this volume.

The conference whose debate gave rise to this volume, "Weapons Threats and International Security: Rebuilding an Unraveled Consensus," is part of a program supported by the Directorate General for Political Affairs of the Italian Ministry of Foreign Affairs, which aims at promoting international debate and raising public awareness on the threats posed by weapons of mass destruction.

The conference, which took place in New York and coincided with Italy's membership, for a two-year mandate, in the UN Security Council, aimed in particular at fostering debate on how to increase the effectiveness of multilateralism in the field of nonproliferation and disarmament, with a view to strengthening international treaties and the agencies in charge of verification of compliance.

Breaking the Nuclear Impasse

New Prospects for Security against Weapons Threats

Edited by
Jeffrey Laurenti and Carl Robichaud

A Century Foundation Book

THE CENTURY FOUNDATION PRESS ▲ NEW YORK

LIBRARY OF CONGRESS CATALOGING-IN-PUBLICATION DATA

Breaking the nuclear impasse : new prospects for security against weapons threats / edited by Jeffrey Laurenti and Carl Robichaud.
 p. cm.
Includes bibliographical references and index.
ISBN 978-0-87078-510-8 (alk. paper)
 1. Nuclear disarmament. 2. Nuclear nonproliferation. 3. Nuclear arms control. I. Laurenti, Jeffrey. II. Robichaud, Carl. III. Title.

JZ5665.B73 2007
327.1'747--dc22   200702561

FOREWORD

When the Italian Ministry of Foreign Affairs contacted The Century Foundation about organizing a conference in New York early in 2007 focused on the prospects for effective action against weapons threats to international security, we were immediately intrigued. Such a conference, we understood, might complement the Italian government's interest in making arms issues a major priority during its two-year term on the United Nations Security Council. For us, however, it was the dramatic changes on these issues that appear to be developing in the United States that made the proposed dialogue especially opportune.

Midterm elections in late 2006 had removed from the chokepoints of congressional power lawmakers who had resisted the comprehensive nuclear test ban treaty in the U.S. Senate in 1998. The officials most vehemently critical of arms control treaties, international inspections, and restraints on (U.S.) nuclear weapons were departing the government. Overall, after a dramatic experiment in repudiation of arms limits, dismissal of weapons inspectors, and enforcement through preventive war, the United States appears to be edging toward more traditionally "realist" policy approaches. The troubled operation in Iraq—formally undertaken as a disarmament policing action by the few with the resolve to act—has reminded Americans of the virtues of international legal obligations, multilateral processes, and military restraint.

With the end of the Cold War, there were hopes that progress on disarmament would proceed in tandem with tight restraint on nuclear, chemical, and biological weapons. While there are positive developments in both areas, the new awareness of the dangers posed by terrorists and others has moved these matters back to the center of international attention.

We are well aware of the challenges that biological, chemical, and nuclear weapons pose to peace and security. But it is useful to remember that we have faced these dangers before—from chemical weapons since 1915, from nuclear weapons since 1945—and over time we have built surprisingly durable international firewalls to contain or eliminate them. Indeed, for all the very real concern we would hear at our conference, "Weapons Threats and International

Security," the bargain that underpins the nonproliferation regime has proved remarkably resilient in limiting the spread of nuclear weapons. The question remains, of course, can it do so in the future.

The Century Foundation, for a half-century, has been involved on issues of nuclear, chemical, and biological weapons. Robert Oppenheimer—the director of the Manhattan Project and tormented father of the atomic bomb—was a trustee of the Foundation. We published early works on nuclear dangers by Thomas Schelling and Morton Halperin. In recent years we have produced influential reports of a task force on biological weapons and an excellent book on nuclear risks, *Ultimate Security*, edited by Janne E. Nolan.

Ultimate Security includes an excellent piece on the successes and failures of the nonproliferation regime by Joseph Cirincione, one of the most trenchant analysts of weapons policy in the United States and the author, most recently, of *Bomb Scare: The History and Future of Nuclear Weapons*. Not only did Cirincione and his colleagues at the Center for American Progress work closely with The Century Foundation in making the conference program a substantive success, but also he has taken the lead, together with The Century Foundation's own rising scholar on nuclear issues, Carl Robichaud, in writing the report that leads off this volume.

The volume you hold in your hands is a product of the debate that occurred at the conference that we organized in New York on February 26, 2007. We turned to half a dozen of the substantive contributors to the conference and asked them to develop some of their keenest observations into essays for a broader audience both in the United States and globally. We are pleased to present here the broad range of ideas and views they offer on how to sustain and enforce the international ban on the use and spread of nuclear weapons. I am grateful to each of the authors for so promptly producing such polished articles.

The full transcript of the conference debate is published online at www.tcf.org, but one particular segment was so precisely focused on perhaps the most urgent immediate flashpoint in the nuclear proliferation debate that we have reproduced it here: a "point/counterpoint" discussion on keeping Iran free of nuclear weapons that featured Richard Haass, the president of the Council on Foreign Relations and a former policymaker in the administrations of both the elder and the younger Presidents Bush, and Javad Zarif, the capable permanent representative of Iran to the United Nations. This is an area in which The Century Foundation became particularly active as signs multiplied over the past year of a looming showdown with Tehran, and the series of white papers the Foundation has commissioned and published have contributed substantially to a clearer public understanding of the many dimensions of this clash.

This volume would not have been possible had it not been for the efforts of Jeffrey Laurenti, senior fellow at The Century Foundation and editor, with Robichaud, of this collection. And of course I must also express our appreciation to the Italian Ministry of Foreign Affairs, including in particular Director-General Giulio Terzi, for its initiative in supporting this work. We hope it helps underscore, for Americans and their international partners alike, the urgency of maintaining a firm and consistent international policy against nuclear weapons.

RICHARD C. LEONE
President, The Century Foundation

Contents

ACKNOWLEDGMENTS

This volume is the work of many individuals. We are indebted of course to the authors, without whom this book would not exist, but also to the many governmental and nongovernmental experts who helped refine the ideas and arguments in these essays, first at an expert planning meeting in Washington and later at a high-profile conference ("Weapons Threats and International Security: Rebuilding an Unraveled Consensus") in New York.

First and foremost, we are grateful to the Italian Ministry of Foreign Affairs and particularly its director-general for multilateral political affairs and human rights, Giulio Terzi di Sant'Agata, whose idea it was to seize this moment of opportunity and whose leadership helped ensure the financial wherewithal that supported this work and the intellectual debate that sharpened it. We are also indebted to Joseph Cirincione for his wisdom, energy, and enthusiasm, as well as to his team at the Center for American Progress, Victoria Suarez-Palomo and Andrew Grotto, who have been substantively and substantially involved from the start. Joe, of course, has made a direct contribution to this volume in its sparkling opening essay.

We also want to acknowledge the several expert participants who lent their time and wisdom in the project's preparatory phase, especially those who contributed strategy memos on which issues should be emphasized as our work unfolded. These individuals include Christopher Chyba and Michael Krepon (both of whom have contributed articles in the present book), Daryl Kimball, Laura Holgate, Alexander Lennon, Michael Levi, Taisuke Mibae, Achilles Emílio Zaluar Neto, Peter Potman, Stan Norris, Randy Rydell, and Frank von Hippel. We further benefited from the advice and counsel of Rand Beers, Wade Boese, Deepti Choubey, Robert Einhorn, Stephen Kull, Miles Pomper, Nicholas Roche, Lawrence Scheinman, Andrew Semmel, Leon Sigal, and Elizabeth Turpen.

The February conference attended by over a hundred expert participants and by a dozen journalists, including CNN and CSPAN, brought lively discussion of these issues to a far broader audience, and we are grateful to them and to the conference speakers and panelists, whose insights stimulated the authors and editors of this volume as they refined their thinking in these papers. Emerson Sykes and Alexandra Kendall deserve special recognition for their support in this process, as does Jason Renker, Century's vice president for publications, whose editorial eye was critical to the final shape of the manuscript. Finally, Carol Starmack and Stephanie Theirl kept the project on time in countless ways. We are grateful to them all.

Jeffrey Laurenti
Carl Robichaud

1.

INTRODUCTION
CLEARING THE NUCLEAR CLOUDS

Jeffrey Laurenti

Addressing doubts about the evidence that Iraq was in fact developing nuclear weapons, White House national security adviser Condoleezza Rice declared in late summer 2002 that "we don't want the smoking gun to be a mushroom cloud."[1] Her argument mirrored the new public anxieties about nuclear weapons dangers in the wake of the World Trade Center attacks—anxieties that had disappeared from public consciousness with the end of the Cold War.

The twenty-first-century anxieties are markedly different, however, from the fears of the Cold War confrontation. The concern during the decades of fevered ideological confrontation had been of devastating nuclear exchanges between abundantly armed superpowers, with strategies of deterrence apparently successful in restraining hawkish instincts on each side by dint of the terrifying prospect of mutually assured destruction. Public anxieties in the era of Dr. Strangelove, marked by air raid drills in schools, strontium-90 in milk, and a proliferation of backyard fallout shelters, quickly subsided after the successful negotiation of the Partial Test Ban Treaty in 1963. A quarter-century later, the end of the Cold War resulted, perhaps paradoxically, in the dismantling not of the nuclear weapons arsenals that the confrontation had spawned, but of the citizen movements for disarmament that had long pressed for their elimination.

The events of September 11, 2001, raised a different specter: after the carnage at the World Trade Center, the possibility that terrorists could obtain nuclear material and inflict catastrophic damage gripped the public imagination.[2] Farsighted political leaders could also see a thread linking a jihadist threat to one posed by modestly sized countries that might acquire nuclear weapons. Whether in the hands of hostile governments or fanatical terrorists, even a few nuclear weapons posed a fearsome threat to countries' national security.

Biological weapons attacks against the U.S. Capitol a month later—anthrax-laced letters whose real return address has never been identified, though the Trenton, New Jersey, postmark was clear enough—exacerbated the public panic. And while the instruments of attack that autumn were decidedly commonplace—box-cutters carried aboard passenger planes, letters dropped into a mailbox—they galvanized far-reaching countermeasures. The post–September 11 security environment provided compelling reasons for robust actions for preparedness that were politically unpersuasive just a month before. The case for abandoning of the 1972 Anti-Ballistic Missile Treaty overnight became politically compelling in Washington, opening the door to deployment of an antimissile system that could, it was hoped, intercept hostile missiles that "rogue" states might launch or supply to terrorists. Eventually, like-minded partners would emerge in East Asia and Eastern Europe to encourage forward deployment against new threats.

At least in the United States, there was little high-level interest in tightening multilateral controls, which were widely thought to be ineffective against America's adversaries but all too constraining of U.S. power. Convinced that powerful nations could best protect their security by acting on their own, rather than by trusting easily paralyzed multilateral mechanisms and talk-shops, U.S. policymakers disavowed the Comprehensive Nuclear Test Ban Treaty, advanced a Proliferation Security Initiative to operate as a posse of willing antinuclear enforcers, sought to avoid formalizing as a legally binding treaty a new U.S.-Russian agreement on nuclear warheads, and—fatefully—judged United Nations weapons inspections incapable of controlling Iraq's unconventional arms development.

Since the United States, more than any other power, sets the pace for progress on international arms policy—a point underscored by several contributors to this volume—a major consequence of the ascent to power in Washington of arms control skeptics was, in terms of international controls, a nuclear freeze—or, perhaps, nuclear weapons policy à la carte, with a sovereign state picking and choosing among negotiated commitments those to which it would still give effect. This would prove, in a very literal sense, unsettling, for what had seemed settled might no longer be.

While the Nuclear Non-Proliferation Treaty (NPT) Review Conference had approved the treaty's indefinite extension in 1995, as well as a thirteen-step program in 2000 toward a nuclear-free world, the first review conference after the September 11 attacks, in 2005, adjourned without agreeing on any policy statement at all, despite the professed anxieties worldwide about nuclear dangers. The default position became, therefore, reliance on national, even unilateral, purpose and action.

What had been a steadily tightening international consensus on nuclear weapons was, publicly and formally, coming unraveled.

The political currents in the United States that pressed most resolutely for vigorous national measures to preempt attacks and rebuild nuclear defenses were the same that had opposed the Partial Test Ban Treaty in 1963, and the Strategic Arms Limitation Treaties of the 1970s, while championing new nuclear weapons development and research into space-based military systems. But they also won support, at least for a while, across much of the U.S. political system after September 11 for their sense of urgency about assertive national action, and for their pessimism about the reliability of multilateral measures. This was manifested not only in considerable bipartisan support for a preventive war against Iraq, but also in a seemingly widespread belief that other major powers, especially Russia and China, are essentially indifferent to the dangers of nuclear proliferation. Their apparent unwillingness to take effective action against sinister governments—"regimes"—that are unmistakably pursuing nuclear weapons programs, such as North Korea and Iran (together with their partner in a tripartite "axis of evil," Iraq before 2003), has convinced many in Washington, and perhaps some in Europe and Japan as well, of the need for national assertiveness.

Yet even within the United States, the political majority for a nuclear policy based on the perceived moral character of the possessor rather than the character of the weapons themselves—sometimes called the "NRA approach" (after the dictum of the National Rifle Association that "guns don't kill people, criminals do")—has proved unstable. Events in the last quarter of 2006 dramatically altered the political landscape on these issues:

- North Korea tested a nuclear device—and the UN Security Council responded with sanctions, imposed with Russia's and China's support;
- Iran's refusal to honor Security Council demands to suspend nuclear enrichment likewise earned it targeted UN sanctions, again with Russian and Chinese support;
- the American electorate installed Democratic majorities in the U.S. Congress, after twelve years of conservative Republican rule; and, perhaps in consequence,
- nuclear fundamentalists began streaming out of the Bush administration, with traditional foreign policy "realists" visibly gaining influence in its policy councils.

Washington's agreement in early 2007 to a pact for control of North Korea's nuclear program was a first concrete sign of the Bush administration's embrace of compromise in the nuclear field.

It now becomes possible to imagine a renewed international consensus on control of nuclear dangers, based on the demonstrated resolve of UN enforcers to penalize proliferators and on a new willingness in Washington to forge compromises with international partners on both means and ends. This sense of emerging opportunities prompted The Century Foundation, with the inspiration and support of the Italian Foreign Ministry and the warm collaboration of Joseph Cirincione and his colleagues at the Center for American Progress, to organize a major international conference on weapons threats to international security and the prospects for rebuilding the unraveled consensus on nuclear policy.

The spirited discussion at the conference—accessible in full on The Century Foundation Web site—prompted further reflections by several leading conference participants, developed as the essays in this volume. Joseph Cirincione, working with The Century Foundation's Carl Robichaud, has captured the sense of the debate at the conference that, just as the severity of the September 11 shock had pushed the United States to seek weapons solutions on its own, impasses such as the troubled enforcement operation in Iraq have prompted Washington's discovery that sustainable solutions require buy-in from, and coordination and even compromise with, others in the international system. Cirincione and Robichaud outline a series of steps that the United States, other nuclear-armed states, and the vast majority of countries eschewing nuclear arms can agree in fairly short order to undertake—even some that the U.S. Congress can take directly in the face of a slower-moving executive branch.

Jayantha Dhanapala recalls the hard bargaining on the interlocking components of the 1995 agreement that included the indefinite extension of the NPT—a top priority of American diplomacy that was by no means a preordained outcome. He suggests that the antinuclear countries had good reason to suspect that the nuclear-armed powers might simply take the non-nuclear states' self-denial for granted as permanent and unconditional while locking in their own arsenals indefinitely. Yet Dhanapala sees signs of a new convergence of interests among leading states in tightening the noose against nuclear use, just at the moment that concerns about global warming have led to renewed debate about possible promotion of nuclear power.

Michael Krepon is even more upbeat. Despite the rocky record of recent years, he counsels, pessimism about successfully managing the nuclear dangers is unwarranted. We have overcome far worse suspicions and entrenched interests that fueled far more dangerous arms races in the Cold War, and the web of national and international controls that has been spun since those days has actually proved quite durable: even the most adamant national sovereigntists in the United States do not propose to abandon the NPT.

Christopher Chyba focuses specifically on American policy as he calls for comprehensive approaches to control of both nuclear and biological weapons. These—in contrast to international policy on chemical weapons—either have effective monitoring but lack uniformity (in the two-tiered rules permitting a few states licitly to hold nuclear arsenals) or show universality in their prohibition but lack monitoring and enforcement (in the existing 1972 Biological Weapons Convention). He argues for measures to stanch both the supply side and the demand side for nuclear weapons production, and calls urgently for steps to cope with biological weapons threats—measures that also would reinforce sound public health policy against the far greater mortality risks of disease pandemics.

William Potter makes the case that what he views as an unsustainable two-tiered nuclear order will become even more unstable if states with active nuclear weapons programs gain access to international markets for "civilian" nuclear technology and supplies. He warns that the already porous wall separating nuclear energy programs from weapons development will become a barrier-free fog with the pending U.S.-India nuclear agreement, unless the agreement is very strictly construed and monitored.

Henry Sokolski is also concerned about the potential to redirect "peaceful" nuclear programs to weapons uses, but suggests a novel reliance on the magic of the marketplace to discourage weapons-prone nuclear programs. He is skeptical of calls to restart nuclear energy promotion under the guise of safeguarding the planet against climate change induced by fossil fuels; the direct and indirect costs of nuclear power are really quite high, he insists—and the enrichment cycle in particular is a constant temptation to security establishments to weaponize. He calls for agreement on a global norm that all forms of energy production operate on a level economic playing field. Withdraw all direct and indirect subsidies from nuclear power, Sokolski argues, and the astronomical true costs of nuclear energy production will quickly snuff out the dangerous proliferation of national nuclear programs masquerading as "peaceful."

In his contribution, Hans Blix underscores the centrality of the "double bargain" linking nonproliferation and disarmament that is at the heart of the NPT regime: we can expect international enforcement of nonproliferation only if the existing holders of nuclear caches move to eliminate them. Blix warns that, absent a deal for total elimination, simplistic proposals to ban enrichment by states that are not recognized weapons holders will be stillborn—not because of Russia or China, but because of objections from the likes of Australia, Brazil, or Canada. He advances proposals to engage the three nuclear-armed holdouts and to reduce nuclear dangers in the Middle East, asserting that "it is not Mars but Venus that will succeed."

Finally, Carl Robichaud offers a vivid portrayal of seeming American policy incoherence on nuclear issues in recent years, and outlines steps the United States can take in short order to break the current impasse in which nuclear-armed states focus on proliferation and the non-nuclear majority focuses on disarmament. He argues that securing nuclear materials, bolstering the credibility of the NPT system among all its constituencies, and dealing directly with hard cases such as North Korea and Iran are all interrelated priorities.

The assembled chapters can accelerate the convergence of positions on international nuclear policy in advance of the 2010 NPT Review Conference, which will be a major opportunity to break the impasse of post–September 11 policy polarization. Arms issues will unavoidably be—either through a narrow lens of enforcement (that is, "Iraq" and "Iran") or a wide-angle lens of global security and the institutions that support it—part of Americans' national conversation culminating in the November 2008 presidential election. These issues will arise in parliamentary and general election debates in a wide range of other countries as well. There is little doubt about the aspirations of the citizenry of all countries: they want a world free of nuclear dangers. The specter of mushroom clouds has once again shaped the national and international security debate. Resolute leadership can clear those clouds away.

2.

INTO THE BREACH

THE DRIVE FOR A NEW GLOBAL NUCLEAR STRATEGY

Joseph Cirincione and Carl Robichaud

"Once more unto the breach, dear friends, once more."
–*Henry V,* William Shakespeare

INTRODUCTION

The world is in a period of significant political transition. By early 2009, four out of the five permanent members of the United Nations Security Council—the United States, Russia, France, and the United Kingdom—will have new executive leadership. Several other major states, including Iran, will likely also change leaders during the next two years. Some, including Germany and Italy, already have. The United Nations has just installed a new secretary-general, and other international bodies, including the International Atomic Energy Agency, also will elect new executives during this period.

This transition presents a unique moment for charting a new course on one of the major threats to global security—the existence of nuclear arsenals and their spread to other nations. "With this leadership change," says former United Nations under-secretary-general of disarmament Jayantha Dhanapala, "it is for us in civil society, to try to urge new perspectives and new opportunities for [world leaders] to seize so that we can make the right choices at the right time."[1]

Dhanapala spoke at a February 2007 conference convened in New York by The Century Foundation with the support of the Center for American Progress and the government of Italy. His perspective, elaborated in this collection of papers commissioned from

9

eight conference participants, was shared in at least one fundamental respect by most at this defining event: the nonproliferation regime is at a critical juncture.

Despite a driving snowstorm, over one hundred top officials and experts from around the world spent the day in deep discussion. With good reason: the decisions taken over the next few years will determine whether we continue the progress of the last two decades of the twentieth century in reducing and eliminating nuclear weapons and programs, or whether the world launches into a second wave of proliferation.

The nonproliferation regime has been more robust than many expected. President John F. Kennedy was not alone when he lamented in 1960 that, instead of the four nations that then had nuclear weapons, there could be twenty or twenty-five nuclear weapon states within a decade. Today, there are still only nine. Though that is too many, with too many weapons, the nuclear world grew at the relatively slow pace of roughly one state per decade. The nuclear dam that Kennedy and his successors from both U.S. political parties worked with international partners to build has largely held. Indeed, more countries have abandoned nuclear weapons programs over the past fifteen years than have tried to acquire them. These were not easy cases: Argentina, Brazil, South Africa, Ukraine, Belarus, Kazakhstan, Iraq, and, most recently, Libya abandoned programs and, in four cases, weapons. No country has commenced a nuclear weapons program since the end of the Cold War. Decisions by India, Libya, Iran, Iraq, Pakistan, and North Korea to pursue nuclear capabilities came well over twenty, thirty, forty years ago.

There also have been positive developments in strengthening current nonproliferation policy tools. Dhanapala and other conference speakers highlighted efforts to boost Cooperative Threat Reduction programs, the passage of UN Security Council Resolution 1540, the Proliferation Security Initiative, the promotion of the Additional Protocol to the International Atomic Energy Agency (IAEA), and the creation of a Central Asian Nuclear Weapon-Free Zone and consolidation of other nuclear-weapon-free zones as examples.[2]

However, it was the events of the past few years that brought this assembly to the meeting room across from the United Nations that cold late winter day and that kept the room filled with debate and participants until the last speaker; it was the fear that new threats were mounting and the nonproliferation regime was unraveling. Barely a week goes by without a new, ominous headline of advancing nuclear programs, nuclear black markets, nuclear terrorism risks, the spread of nuclear material production capabilities, or stalemates at disarmament talks. Former UN secretary-general Kofi Annan reflected the expert consensus when he warned in 2005 of a new "cascade of proliferation."[3] The failure of the Nonproliferation Treaty Review Conference that year to adopt a final declaration was viewed by some as a near-death knell for the multilateral consensus on established nonproliferation norms.

There is nothing inevitable, however, about either proliferation or the decline of the regime. "It has been a lot worse and we bounced back," said Michael Krepon of the Henry L. Stimson Center, "and we can bounce back again." Proliferation problems looked terrible in 1949 after the Soviet Union became the second nuclear nation, Krepon noted at the conference, with the United States "clearly headed into a terrible arms race with a sworn ideological foe."[4] Even in 1962, when the United States held a roughly twenty-to-one advantage in nuclear arms, the Cuban missile crisis nearly tipped into a nuclear holocaust. China's fevered revolutionary rhetoric about surviving nuclear war and promoting nuclear proliferation in the early 1960s prompted hardliners in the United States to urge a nuclear preemptive strike. But cooler heads contained and rolled back many of these dangers and we emerged from the Cold War without the use of any nuclear weapons in combat—a feat many thought impossible.

No one underestimates the difficulties and setbacks of the past few years. "Yet, despite these disappointments," said the Italian Foreign Ministry director of disarmament and nonproliferation, Filippo Formica, "the principles which underpin the nonproliferation regime have never actually been challenged." This, he concluded, "indicates that the NPT [Non-Proliferation Treaty] continues to be considered the cornerstone of international disarmament and nonproliferation."[5]

Indeed, there are signs of a revived momentum for control of nuclear weapons. Several of the conference speakers pointed to the importance of the joint January *Wall Street Journal* editorial by former secretaries of state George Shultz and Henry Kissinger, former secretary of defense William Perry, and former chairman of the Senate Armed Services Committee Sam Nunn. The editorial, with its un-

abashed call for a phase-out of nuclear weapons, represents a significant change in the thinking of influential policy and decision makers
in the United States and other nuclear weapons states. "First and foremost," said Dhanapala, "they talk of intensive work with the leaders
of the countries in possession of nuclear weapons to turn the goal of a
world without nuclear weapons into a joint enterprise." Most agreed
that the heavy lifting has to begin with the nuclear weapons states.
Hans Blix, chair of the International Commission on Weapons of
Mass Destruction, argued that it would be difficult to "turn the tide"
unless there is a change of attitude in the nuclear weapons states.
"They should take the lead for significant disarmament," he said.[6]

Director Formica noted that the Italian government was focus-
ing on three concrete steps toward such an approach: (1) making the
Additional Protocol a condition of nuclear technology supply; (2) negotiation of a treaty to cut off the production of fissile material for
weapons; and (3) finally bringing into force the Comprehensive Test
Ban Treaty (CTBT). Others articulated their own priority plans, including calls for a "no first test" pledge, prevention of an arms race in
outer space, and a crash program to eliminate nuclear terrorism. We
summarize below the nine steps with the broadest conference support,
grouped into those that decrease the demand for these weapons by reducing the drivers of nuclear proliferation and those that decrease the
supply of these weapons by raising the barriers to their acquisition.

Throughout the conference debate there was a sober assessment
of the challenges, coupled with an urgent assertion of the need to
forge a new global consensus. Princeton University's Christopher
Chyba urged the United States and others to grapple with tough
"nuclear tradeoffs" and develop a "nuclear weapons policy that provides a comprehensive approach to managing nuclear risk." Former
U.S. Representative Jim Leach recalled Einstein's warning that split-
ting the atom had changed everything except our way of thinking,
and argued that the dangers posed by nuclear weapons required a
new approach: "If there is any period in history when the case for
advancing international laws could conceivably be greater, I don't
know when it would be."[7]

It would be going too far to say the participants were optimistic,
but there was not one that called for retreat from the battle. As King
Henry V told his men, "when the blast of war blows in our ears" it
is time to "bend every spirit." The game's afoot.

A Consensus Plan of Action

If policymakers approach the challenges we face purposefully—neither lulled into complacency, nor paralyzed by pessimism—there are many steps that can be taken today that would immediately enhance global security.

Several participants at the conference argued that there is little dispute over what actions must be taken. A list of valuable steps "is not difficult at all to draw up," noted Hans Blix, whose Weapons of Mass Destruction Commission report presented sixty specific recommendations. "The list can be made very long," he observed, "but the main thing is the turn of the tide."[8]

This is not to suggest that implementing these steps will be easy: serious debates remain over how to sequence actions and what rights and responsibilities are conferred by each arrangement. Nevertheless, there is wide if not universal agreement that our goal must be a world in which nuclear weapons cannot be used. While there remains contentious debate over how to get there, there has emerged a remarkable degree of consensus about where we need to go.

The Special Role of the United States

Many of these steps focus on the United States and Russia, which together possess ninety-six percent of the world's nuclear weapons and whose actions set the tone for nuclear diplomacy.

Among the expert participants at the conference there was no disagreement that the United States is uniquely now the driver of international nuclear policy. This is not just because of America's preeminent military and economic power, its control of roughly half of the world's nuclear arsenal, or its disproportionate influence among world powers. It is also because the United States has, at virtually every juncture, shaped the international rules and norms of the nonproliferation regime and led the negotiations to form the NPT and the Nuclear Suppliers Group.

The United States long stood as the champion of a legal order constraining the acquisition and use of nuclear weapons, despite pressures in some quarters to normalize them. "During the entire administration of Dwight David Eisenhower, the United States was not on the losing side of any U.N. vote," noted Jim Leach. "By contrast, in this administration, on ten articles relating to arms control, the United States was the only vote in opposition." It is the sense that the United States is turning its back on long-standing commitments that has led many to question whether the one-time consensus upholding the nonproliferation regime is unraveling.

In order to reverse this trend, the United States needs to develop a comprehensive approach to managing nuclear risks. The United States should focus the greatest government resources on the most serious threats: preventing nuclear terrorism, blocking the emergence of new nuclear states, reducing the dangers from existing arsenals, and fortifying the nonproliferation regime. U.S. nonproliferation policies should maximize the barriers to proliferation while minimizing the drivers of proliferation.

Policies to maximize the barriers to proliferation would increase the political cost of violating global nonproliferation norms, increase the difficulty of acquiring nuclear technology, and raise the direct and indirect costs of acquiring nuclear weapons.

Policies to minimize the drivers would reduce the security factors driving states to acquire nuclear weapons and reduce the prestige associated with these weapons.

The conference focused heavily on identifying concrete steps. In this report we discuss nine feasible actions, grouped into two categories: four that set up *barriers* to proliferation, four that address the *drivers* to proliferation, and one that addresses both.

CREATING BARRIERS TO PROLIFERATION

Prevent Nuclear Terrorism

The greatest priority for preventing a nuclear catastrophe is securing loose nuclear material, primarily in the former Soviet Union. American participants particularly focused on this threat and warned of the nation's continued vulnerability. "We've been lucky, but we can't count on that luck," said Dr. William Potter, director of the Center for Nonproliferation Studies.

Several programs, such as Cooperative Threat Reduction, are under way to bolster controls on these materials by working with

Russia to upgrade safeguards on its nuclear facilities. However, these programs have been permitted to languish with insufficient funding and lack high-level leadership and coordination among Russian and American agencies.

Reform the Fuel Cycle

The NPT allows states access to a full nuclear fuel cycle, including technologies and know-how that can translate into military use. Among participants, there was a consensus that we need to close this proliferation "loophole." Hans Blix noted, however, that many of the diplomatic and technical details are not yet in place: the U.S.-proposed Global Nuclear Energy Partnership (GNEP) "is ingenious but it lies twenty years in the future." As for immediate solutions, he noted that the IAEA panel tasked with finding a solution could not reach consensus, and was stymied by questions of how to ensure that fuel supply is not politicized. "Who will decide," he asked, "whether Venezuela can buy fuel for a research reactor or not?"

Plans for a multilateral fuel bank must both ensure supply and end perceptions that the real goal is to perpetuate a two-tier world of a few nuclear weapon "haves" vigorously defending their power versus a large number of nuclear weapons "have nots."

End Production of Fissile Material

Despite international efforts, there remains no treaty banning nuclear states from producing material for nuclear weapons. Cutting off fissile production is a critical step toward reinforcing international nonproliferation norms and disarmament goals. In fact, as Fillippo Formica of Italy noted, "for over ten years there has been a substantial agreement in the main international fora on the value that the Fissile Material Cutoff Treaty (FMCT) would give to the nuclear non-proliferation cause."

Negotiations over the FMCT have stalled because states have sought to link their participation to gains on other issues or have questioned the efficacy of the treaty. China, for example, has made its support of the FMCT conditional, using the treaty as a bargaining chip to bring the United States to the table for negotiations on a treaty to prevent an arms race in space. Meanwhile, the

Bush administration in 2004 announced that it would not support verification measures in a future FMCT, arguing that the necessary inspection regime would be too expensive and costly.

This is a dangerous approach, since constituencies within several states are pressing to restart fissile production. On the other hand, if nuclear states outside the NPT (India, Pakistan, Israel, and North Korea) could be persuaded to join such a fissile material regime, the treaty could begin to set limits on the nuclear activities of these states. There was significant consensus among those at the conference that, in the words of Formica, "the time has come to upgrade the level of international commitment toward an FMCT."

Universalize the Additional Protocol

IAEA safeguards remain circumscribed, with the agency essentially limited to verifying and monitoring declared activities. Clandestine programs in Iraq and North Korea exposed the vulnerability of this arrangement.

The Additional Protocol would help fill this gap. Without this additional authority, the IAEA is like a policeman with a warrant to search every room of a house—except the basement. Gustavo Zlauvinen of the IAEA noted that ensuring a "high level of credibility will depend on the legal authority," and "the additional protocol is a very important element for us to increase that legal authority."

DECREASING THE PROLIFERATION DRIVERS

Reaffirm the Goal of the Elimination of Nuclear Weapons

The United States has reduced its arsenal to the lowest levels since the 1950s but has received little credit for these cuts because they were conducted in isolation from a commitment to disarmament. At the conference, participants argued that the failure of the nuclear powers, and especially the United States, to accept their end of the NPT bargain was undermining every other aspect of the nonproliferation agenda.

The United States should re-reaffirm that nuclear weapons have no role in today's world, except perhaps to deter other nuclear weapons, and it should promise not to use nuclear weapons first in any conflict. There is no expectation that the United States will disarm its nuclear arsenal tomorrow, or without a system in place to secure a nuclear-free world. But a "no first use" pledge is critical to charting a course away from reliance on nuclear arms. Russia, India, and China have all made such a pledge in the past, and the United States and the other nuclear states should join them.

De-alert U.S. and Russian Forces

Few people are aware that America and Russia retain thousands of weapons on hair-trigger alert, ready to be launched at a moment's notice. Serious nuclear accidents have happened before and can happen again, especially as Soviet early warning systems continue to erode. Dhanapala described de-alerting U.S. and Russian forces as an "urgent step which would lay the groundwork for a world free of nuclear threat."

The United States should take immediate action, unilaterally or in concert with Russia, to de-alert its nuclear arsenal. Stepping back from high alert could be accomplished quickly and inexpensively and entails no real risks, since each side remains assured of a second-strike capability. The new posture would both reduce risks and signal a shift away from reliance on nuclear deterrence.

Remove and Eliminate Tactical Nuclear Weapons

Tactical weapons pose the most alluring targets for theft by terrorists or criminal networks. Despite this, the 2002 Moscow agreement negotiated by Presidents Bush and Putin was silent on tactical weapons.

This was a missed opportunity to remove the 150 to 450 tactical nuclear weapons that are stationed in eight European states. Russia is more ambivalent about the utility of its tactical arms, but could be persuaded to dismantle parts of its arsenal as a quid pro quo.

Participants agreed that these weapons should be decommissioned, but there was discussion over whether the United States might move to do so unilaterally or as part of a package arrangement with Russia. Pugwash's Paolo Cotta-Ramusino argued for the removal of nuclear weapons from other countries' soil and for the reduction and increased control of Russia's massive tactical arsenal—"they should be put together in a way which is constructive, not wait too much for one to be solved in order to solve the other one."

Consistently Enforce Nonproliferation Norms

One of the most persistent themes voiced by participants was the need for consistent interpretation of nonproliferation commitments. Participants were critical in particular of the recent India-United States deal, which would provide assistance to India's nuclear program even in the absence of full safeguards. "I think there has always been this fallacy that there can be safe hands for nuclear weapons and unsafe hands," said Dhanapala. "We are losing sight of the inherent dangers of this weapon itself" when policymakers and commentators draw a distinction between their acquisition by democracies and their acquisition by non-democracies.

William Potter said that "we must do everything possible to reward good nonproliferation behavior, rather than to devalue non-nuclear weapons state membership in the NPT. And I think the U.S.-India deal does precisely the opposite." Henry Sokolski, director of the Nonproliferation Policy Education Center, noted that we have already seen some consequences of making exceptions: "I've heard the Pakistani officials go 180 degrees, saying, 'OK, it's not that bad. Now give us the same treatment.'"

Ratify the Comprehensive Test Ban Treaty

There was one step mentioned by conference participants that affects both the supply and demand side of nuclear weapon: bringing into force the Comprehensive Test Ban Treaty. Formica noted the European consensus that "the CTBT would be an important contribution to international peace and security." The treaty makes it more difficult for new nuclear weapons states to develop weapons and for existing nuclear powers to expand their arsenals. Moreover, the CTBT is seen as a litmus test of commitment to eventual nuclear disarmament. Ratifying the test ban would cost the United States virtually nothing, but have tremendous benefits.

While the agenda focused on regime-wide issues, in the background of these discussions was the Iran question, and participants frequently alluded to the intensifying confrontation. This discussion came to the forefront during the lunch debate between Richard Haass, president of the Council on Foreign Relations, and Ambassador Javad Zarif, permanent representative of Iran to the United Nations, which was moderated by Carla Anne Robbins of the *New York Times*. This conversation offered a rare on-the-record exchange between a high-ranking Iranian negotiator and a former high-ranking official in the Bush administration. The transcript of this discussion is reprinted in full in this volume.

FROM "WHAT" TO "HOW"

The steps advocated above would increase global security but will not be easy to implement. Today the challenge for the arms control community is to move from a list of "desirables" and toward a political plan to realize them—moving from the "what" to the "how," as Michael Krepon put it. In doing so, leaders will need to find formulas that simultaneously meet the demands of domestic constituencies and international negotiating partners. The chapters in this volume are particularly promising because they suggest ways to satisfy these demands and operationalize an agenda that too often remains abstract. These practical steps offer a concrete agenda for increased security and cooperation.

3.

REBUILDING AN UNRAVELED CONSENSUS FOR SUSTAINABLE NONPROLIFERATION

Jayantha Dhanapala[1]

SOME INCONVENIENT TRUTHS

Inconvenient truths must sometimes wait their moment. Al Gore may not have won the United States presidential election with his message in 2000, but his recent Oscar for *An Inconvenient Truth* offers some encouragement.

There are many "inconvenient truths" in the international peace and security area that we must confront honestly. The Chicago-based *Bulletin of the Atomic Scientists* recently moved its Doomsday Clock forward two minutes, placing it now at five minutes to midnight. The rationale was that, in addition to the threat of nuclear danger, the world faces another catastrophic danger from climate change.

Last year, a high-level report by a team in the United Kingdom headed by Sir Nicholas Stern reviewed the economic consequences of climate change and foresaw a major global economic downturn comparable to the Great Depression of 1929.[2] This was followed by the report of the Intergovernmental Panel on Climate Change (IPCC), which asserted that global change would most likely lead to a temperature rise of between 1.8°C and 4°C by the end of the century; a sea level rise by 28–43 centimeters; a disappearance of Arctic summer sea ice in the second half of this century; and an increase in heat waves and in tropical storm intensity.[3] The report found these consequences as incontrovertible, and described them as "very likely" to be caused by human actions, and in particular by greenhouse gas emissions.

The forces of globalization and the feverish pursuit of industrialization have led to a vast demand for energy. With environmental concerns already being cited to justify an increasing reliance on nuclear power as an energy source, we must resolve the concerns that wider use of nuclear energy may lead to a proliferation of nuclear weapons. Thus are the two greatest threats to human security, as identified by the *Bulletin of the Atomic Scientists*, inextricably intertwined.

Another inconvenient truth is that we live in a world of escalating military budgets, despite the absence of antagonisms between major states. According to the Stockholm International Peace Research Institute (SIPRI), global military expenditure is at $1,118 billion ($1.1 trillion) per annum, with the United States accounting for 48 percent of the total. In a world where over one billion human beings live below the poverty line of one dollar a day, weapons spending amounts to $173 per year for every man, woman, and child on the planet. Among the world's eight known nuclear-armed states—five of them parties to the Nuclear Non-Proliferation Treaty (NPT)— there remain an estimated 27,000 nuclear weapons, of which 12,000 are actively deployed.[4]

Nuclear weapons are designed to cause terror and destruction on a vastly greater scale than any conventional weapon, killing thousands in a single attack and leaving behind ecological and genetic effects that can persist indefinitely. The risk that these nuclear weapons will be used—by states or terrorists, by accident or design—has actually increased in recent years. This threat, combined with the certainty of climate change, presents an ominous dual challenge to humanity.

But exhorting against complacency is not a counsel to despair. From Jared Diamond's impressive book, *Collapse*,[5] I draw the lesson that, throughout history, not all societies facing imminent danger have failed. With long-term planning and a willingness to reconsider core values, even societies at extreme risk are able to avert collapse.

Globalization and the information and technological revolution have made our challenges more complex, but also offer us tools to assess and mitigate the problems we have created. Along with our scientific advances, our advances in governance—embodied in international institutions and international law—provide us mechanisms to coordinate the collective action that is needed to rid the world of weapons of mass destruction and take corrective action on climate change.

I believe that, at least in the security field, the disastrous policies that have brought us to this point of crisis have run their course. The recent agreement to take collective action in the Security Council to roll back the nuclear program of the Democratic People's Republic of Korea (DPRK), and the Koreans' ultimate accommodation, is a signal that, in politics, practical diplomacy can and does yield results. So too was the Libya case, in which diplomacy and engagement helped end a decades-long weapon program. These results were long overdue, but they point to what can be achieved in other areas—an especially important reminder when military strikes are still contemplated as an approach to fighting proliferation, notwithstanding the lessons of Iraq.

The Unraveling of the Consensus

In 1995 I was privileged to preside over the NPT Review and Extension Conference. The NPT contained a provision for its extension twenty-five years after it came into force and required a majority decision of the states parties to decide on the length of the extension.

The conference was expected to be contentious and complex, and in the post-Cold War climate many states had heightened expectations of far-reaching results. The nuclear weapon states made it clear that they wanted an indefinite extension of the NPT and argued, as we now know disingenuously, that it was an essential prerequisite for nuclear disarmament. They were supported by the Western Group (from North America, Europe, Japan, and Australia) and the Eastern Group (eastern European countries, including the Russian Federation). Once these groups made unconditional extension a high-priority foreign policy goal, the arguments advanced for this outcome became curiously less important than the gathering of the necessary votes.

While a large majority of states represented at the conference favored indefinite extension of the treaty, delegations were nevertheless emphatic that extension was not a carte blanche for nuclear weapons states and insisted that concrete steps be specified in the final document. About halfway through the conference, support began to coalesce around a South African proposal that called for both a strengthened review process and a Declaration of Principles on Nuclear Non-proliferation and Disarmament as a "yardstick" to measure substantive progress. Late in the consultations, a coalition of Arab states successfully advocated a specific resolution calling for respect of the treaty in the Middle East and acceptance of International Atomic Energy Agency (IAEA) safeguards on nuclear facilities in the region.

Ultimately, the package of three inter-related decisions—indefinite extension, strengthened review process, and the "yardsticks" of the Principles and Objectives—together with a resolution on the Middle East was adopted as a package without a vote by the states parties. (I discuss the details of these negotiations in more detail in a separate account.[6])

The adoption of this package had the effect of extending the NPT indefinitely, with clear guidelines for introducing a strengthened review process and with Principles and Objectives to serve as benchmarks for the performance of states parties. Successes in the period immediately following the extension—notably the signature of the Comprehensive Nuclear Test Ban Treaty (CTBT) in 1996 and the expansion of the NPT's membership to 187—seemed to vindicate the decision. The nuclear weapon tests of China and France in the mid-1990s, which were widely condemned, were followed by signature of the CTBT by these two countries and, in the case of France, by its ratification as well.

The indefinite extension was achieved largely because the long-stalled comprehensive test ban—generally seen as the litmus test of nuclear disarmament—seemed at last certain of adoption, and because of the promise by the nuclear weapon states that negotiations would follow for a convention banning the production of fissile material and for a program of nuclear disarmament leading to the elimination of nuclear weapons. In particular, as the *Washington Post* documented in a six-part series in April 1995, the U.S. decision to end nuclear tests and to negotiate a comprehensive test ban, steps that had been advocated by the Non-Aligned Movement (NAM) in previous review conferences, was crucial to the success of the 1995 extension. For this reason, the United States Senate's rejection of CTBT ratification in 1998 struck a blow at the heart of the pact for indefinite extension and triggered the process of unraveling the consensus achieved in 1995. Though the consensus was formally re-iterated at the next review conference in 2000, it was already under strain before the change of personnel and attitudes in the U.S. executive branch early the next year.

Developments outside the NPT also would contribute to this unraveling. In May 1998 India announced the conduct of tests of nuclear devices and was followed soon after by Pakistan. Although neither country was a member of the NPT or the CTBT,[7] these tests were clearly a setback to the prevailing nuclear nonproliferation and disarmament norms, were widely condemned, most notably in UN Security Council Resolution 1172, and triggered limited sanctions by the United States and other Western countries. Today, one may note the contrast between the strong language in that resolution and the terms of the 2006 U.S.-India nuclear cooperation deal—a disparity that vividly illustrates the inconsistent application of nonproliferation norms. George Perkovic has cogently argued that the "democratic bomb" strategy—approval of nuclear weapons in the hands of countries with assertedly democratic government, and disapproval when possessed by other "regimes"—is inherently contradictory and cannot succeed; when the central problem is the weapons themselves, any distinction between "good proliferators" and "bad proliferators" cannot be sustained.[8] Henry Kissinger, recently discussing the case of Iran, wrote that "it is the fact not the provenance of further proliferation that needs to be resisted. . . . We should oppose nuclear proliferation even to a democratic Iran."[9]

A further contrast is the differential punishment meted out in instances of proven proliferation—despite the stringent conditions of UN Security Council Resolution 1540, which was adopted to prevent nonstate actors and terrorist groups from acquiring weapons of mass destruction. The 1540 Committee, which is comprised of all Security Council members, was tasked with monitoring member states' compliance with Resolution 1540. Enforcement, however, has been inconsistent. Recent revelations into the workings of A. Q. Khan's illicit trafficking network—which were well known to Western intelligence agencies for some time—resulted in a mere three convictions and relatively light jail sentences. Numerous other instances of the theft, illegal trafficking, and smuggling of nuclear material have been detected in the post–September 11 atmosphere of heightened concern over international terrorism. Yet in many countries the punishment for these violators is no greater than that for corrupt businessmen or prolific Internet "spammers."

Despite the setbacks to the NPT regime after 1995, the Review Conference of 2000 was a remarkable success due largely to the energetic efforts of a group of countries drawn from different regional groups that called themselves "The New Agenda Coalition." Their firm pressure, and the aversion of the nuclear powers to an open rupture, resulted in the adoption of a final document that contained thirteen specific and practical steps for nuclear disarmament. These steps have become the centerpiece for those committed to the success of the NPT. Subsequent failure by nuclear states to achieve them, despite commitments made at the 2000 Review Conference, has led to the further unraveling of the consensus and a mood of disillusionment.

In fact, instead of implementing the promised thirteen steps, leading nuclear-armed states have reversed the progress of earlier years. Arms control agreements, such as the 1972 Anti-Ballistic Missile treaty (ABM), were abrogated. The Strategic Offensive Reductions Treaty (SORT) between the United States and the Russian Federation, while a gesture toward nuclear disarmament, was deliberately silent on issues of verification and on actual destruction of weapons.

Moreover, the de-emphasis on nuclear weapons in the security doctrines of the major powers after the Cold War has now been replaced by a fresh salience. This was evident in the 2002 Nuclear Posture Review by the United States, and in the reversal by the Russian Federation of its policy of no first use of nuclear weapons against non-nuclear weapon states. Thus a taboo even during the Cold War was now being pronounced as policy. Reviving the prospect of nuclear escalation violates commitments made in 1995 and 2000, and ignores principles of proportional response enshrined in international law and expressly affirmed in the Advisory Opinion of the International Court of Justice in 1996.[10] Meanwhile, concepts of deterrence have spread to South Asia and are invoked by both India and Pakistan to justify their nuclear arsenals as militarily necessary.

The United States, with its planned "bunker buster" weapons and the Reliable Replacement Warhead, reflects this new reliance on nuclear weapons as an active element of military strategy, a development that dangerously lowers the threshold for nuclear use. Russia's President Putin, in a speech in Munich on February 10, 2007, hinted at withdrawal from the Intermediate Range Nuclear Forces Treaty

(INF) and the Treaty on Conventional Armed Forces in Europe (CFE), two important achievements after the Cold War, citing threats to the security of his country. Thus, by words and by deeds, is manifest a fraying relationship between the two powers that possess the majority of nuclear weapons in the world.

Although talks between the two nations are said to have begun in order to prepare for the expiration of disarmament agreements between them in 2009 and 2012, success in these negotiations should not be a foregone conclusion. U.S. plans to deploy components of a missile defense system in Poland and the Czech Republic are seen as a provocation and a break from prior promises. Together with China's launch of an anti-satellite weapon in space, these are ominous signs of a fresh arms race.

In the United Kingdom, a Labour government won parliamentary approval to replace the Trident nuclear submarine system at a cost of $40 billion, up to 3 percent of its annual defense budget for thirty years. Meanwhile the Geneva-based Conference on Disarmament (CD) remains deadlocked and is unable to move on vital issues such as the Fissile Material Cutoff Treaty, negative security assurances, and the prevention of an arms race in outer space—let alone on eliminating nuclear weapons. The failure of the Western nuclear weapon states to ratify the protocols of certain nuclear weapon-free zones is another drawback—it is to the credit of the five Central Asian states that they concluded the Central Asia Nuclear Weapon-free Zone (CANWFZ) in September 2006 in defiance of heavy pressure from the United States, the United Kingdom, and France.

While these setbacks to the process of nuclear disarmament continued, there have been setbacks in the nonproliferation field as well, of which Iraq represents the central case. Iraq's clandestine development of a nuclear weapons program effectively was destroyed after the first Gulf war under Security Council Resolutions 687 and others, and through actions implemented by the IAEA, UNSCOM, and UNMOVIC. Yet this success, painstakingly achieved through a decade of multilateral action, was not apparent; faulty intelligence and allegations that the program still existed led, *inter alia*, to the ruinous invasion of Iraq, despite the failure to find evidence to prove these allegations. The war's results have exposed the limitations of counter-proliferation measures.

The DPRK case is more difficult to assess. When first brought to the attention of the Security Council, it was deflected to a negotiation process that ended in the Agreed Framework in 1994. That agreement was inadequately implemented, and as the Bush administration adopted a truculent attitude to the DPRK, the situation worsened until North Korea, which had announced its withdrawal from the NPT, tested a nuclear weapon in 2006.

That act of proliferation created a sense of urgency and triggered Security Council sanctions. The six-nation talks convened by China finally reached an agreement, announced on February 13, 2007. However, the implementation of the agreement requires regular supervision so that it does not go the way of the earlier Agreed Framework.

Finally there is the continuing case of Iran, whose violation of the IAEA safeguards agreement has led to deep suspicions that its plans for nuclear power may lead to a nuclear weapons program. This has been compounded by Iran's noncompliance with UN Security Council Resolution 1737, barring its enrichment of uranium. There is no doubt that the problem cannot be resolved unilaterally and requires a political and diplomatic process in which all sides must cooperate and compromise.

Dismal as the current global situation may be, it is useful to remind ourselves that we have not arrived at the nightmare scenario envisioned by the late president John F. Kennedy, who foresaw a situation of twenty to twenty-five nuclear armed states. The overwhelming majority of countries that are in the NPT genuinely believe that nuclear weapon possession is not in their security interest. However, as recent events have shown, the existence of a two-tier world of nuclear haves and have-nots cannot be sustained.

Still, there have been some positive nonproliferation developments as well. Libya announced that it was abandoning its own programs of developing weapons of mass destruction, a remarkable success of quiet diplomacy. A number of steps have been taken to tackle the problem of nuclear proliferation, such as the Co-operative Threat Reduction Initiative pioneered by U.S. Senators Dick Lugar and Sam Nunn, the Global Threat Reduction Initiative, the Proliferation Security Initiative, and the Additional Protocols of the IAEA. While these steps can contribute to security, they cannot, separately or together, stem the tide of nuclear proliferation that arises from the continuing political and military value attached to nuclear weapons.

The incontrovertible fact is that nuclear disarmament and nuclear nonproliferation have a symbiotic relationship. They are mutually reinforcing. We cannot have progress in one without progress in the other. The NPT must be viewed in its totality. No one aspect can be singled out for implementation without upsetting the fundamental equilibrium that exists among the nonproliferation, disarmament, and peaceful uses of nuclear energy components of the treaty.

THE WEAPONS OF MASS DESTRUCTION COMMISSION

The accumulation of the setbacks mentioned above made inevitable the failure of the NPT Review Conference of 2005 to achieve an agreed Final Document. Perhaps worse was the failure in September 2005 of the sixtieth anniversary UN General Assembly session to agree on mentioning *any* disarmament issue in its Outcome Document. This surely represents the nadir in the unraveling of the consensus.

It is in response to these intractable challenges that, in my final year as UN under-secretary-general, I proposed an international commission on weapons of mass destruction. Secretary-General Kofi Annan was not ready to have such a commission function under the aegis of the United Nations at a time when relations with its largest member state over such security issues were particularly tense. Sweden, thanks to its courageous foreign minister, the late Anna Lindh, accepted the challenge and set up the commission, with Dr. Hans Blix as chairman.

The members of the commission—fourteen of us, drawn from different countries, including nuclear weapon states—began our work early in 2004. We met in different capitals and exchanged ideas with scholars, researchers, and diplomats from a wide range of countries over a period of more than two years. Finally, in June 2006, we presented the final report to Secretary-General Annan, and it was tabled as a document of the United Nations. Blix also spoke to the First Committee of the United Nations in October 2006 and has tirelessly traveled the globe addressing audiences and media conferences.

Our commission felt that the time for action on weapons of mass destruction, and especially on nuclear weapons, has come. We see them as inhumane weapons of terror—weapons in fact intended most of all to intimidate those who do not possess them. As the Canberra Commission, upon which I also served, said in 1996, "Nuclear weapons are held by a handful of states which insist that these weapons provide unique security benefits and yet reserve uniquely to themselves the right to own them. This situation is highly discriminatory and thus unstable; it cannot be sustained. The possession of nuclear weapons by any state is a constant stimulus to other states to acquire them."[11] The WMD Commission reiterates this, adding that "So long as any such weapons remain in any state's arsenal, there is a high risk that they will one day be used, by design or accident. Any such use would be catastrophic."[12]

Nuclear weapons must be devalued as the ultimate currency of power. That can be achieved only by their elimination. A cooperative rule-based world order requires us to have a nuclear ban negotiated and administered through a multilateral institution. For this purpose we must convene a World Summit that will discuss WMD and agree on a program of action.

A total of sixty recommendations have been made in the WMD Commission Report. They include:

- gaining agreement on general principles, with action on disarmament and nonproliferation through multilateral institutions in a rule-based international order where the UN Security Council is the ultimate authority;
- reviving disarmament negotiations and affirming policies that give states the confidence that they have no need to acquire WMD;
- reducing the danger of existing arsenals by making deep reductions in them; the need to take weapons off their alert status;
- securing weapons and nuclear material from theft, especially by terrorist groups;
- preventing proliferation through the entry into force of the CTBT; the implementation of commitments of the nuclear-weapon states under the NPT; encouraging nuclear weapon-free zones, especially in the Middle East;
- continuing negotiations with DPRK and Iran to ensure their non-nuclear weapon status while assuring them of their security and their right to the peaceful uses of nuclear energy; developing international arrangements for the supply of enriched uranium fuel and disposal of spent fuel;

- working purposefully for a ban on nuclear weapons within a reasonable time frame; prohibiting the production of fissionable material; gaining no-first-use pledges by those who have nuclear weapons; and
- achieving the universalization of the Chemical Weapons Convention and the Biological Weapons Convention, and a legal framework to prevent an arms race in outer space.

NEW OPPORTUNITIES TO REBUILD THE NPT CONSENSUS

A global consensus on disarmament, utopian and elusive as it may seem, has in fact been achieved many times in the past. On January 24, 1946, the UN General Assembly adopted its first resolution calling for the elimination of all atomic weapons and "all other major weapons adaptable to mass destruction." Later, in 1978, the First Special Session of the UN General Assembly devoted to disarmament (SSOD I) agreed on a consensus Final Document that represents what is still the highest watermark of agreement on the entire range of disarmament issues and has never been surpassed. In 1996, with the sole exception of India, a consensus was also achieved on the CTBT. A bilateral consensus that "nuclear war cannot be won and must never be fought" was reached between Presidents Reagan and Gorbachev as a prelude to agreements on nuclear disarmament.

To be sure, such consensus has depended on a convergent political will among the leaders of the most powerful states, which all have elements of their security establishment that are deeply invested in nuclear arms. There are signs that, given the seriousness of the challenges confronting the international community, we may be able to go back to restoring this consensus as a step toward negotiating nuclear disarmament agreements and buttressing the NPT.

On January 4 the *Wall Street Journal* published a remarkable op-ed piece written by George Shultz, William Perry, Henry Kissinger, and Sam Nunn—all former holders of high office in the United States, all highly influential today. They called for "reversing reliance on nuclear weapons globally" and viewed the doctrine of nuclear deterrence as obsolete, increasingly hazardous, and decreasingly effective.[13] Recalling past efforts to rid the world of nuclear weapons, they called for a rekindling of the Reagan-Gorbachev vision and the achievement of a nuclear-weapon-free world as a "joint enterprise." Identifying a series of agreed and urgent steps, the four included many of the measures featured in the thirteen steps of the 2000 NPT Review Conference and the sixty recommendations of the WMD Commission. The article was followed a few days later in the same newspaper by an article by former Soviet president Gorbachev endorsing the four Americans' views and also calling for a dialogue between the nuclear weapon states and non-nuclear weapon states within the framework of the NPT on the elimination of nuclear weapons.

A breakthrough in reconstructing the fractured consensus must come through the political leadership of key countries. Public opinion—especially in democracies—can force policy changes through the electoral process, and civil society organizations must work relentlessly to achieve this.

In the next twenty months, four of the five nuclear weapon states in the NPT are due to change their longstanding political leadership. This provides a unique opportunity for a change of policy on nuclear weapons. First, the presidential election in France this spring (although the nuclear issue was not among the subjects being debated in the campaign); in the United Kingdom, Prime Minister Blair will step down in the course of this year; in 2008, both the Russian Federation and the United States will have elections for a new president. This virtually simultaneous change in the political leadership of key countries will provide an opportunity in the post–Cold War world to make fundamental changes that can pull the world back from the brink.

This new setting could be perfect for pursuing Recommendation 59 of the WMD Commission, which urges the convening of a world summit on the disarmament, nonproliferation, and terrorist use of weapons of mass destruction. The date for such a summit should be in 2009, providing thorough preparation and an opportunity for new leaders to take their seats. Such a summit would represent a historic moment for the world to prove that in this era of globalization we recognize the dangers to our global society and will take the right decisions at the right moment so that the world we live in can be a world future generations can live with.

4.

NUCLEAR PESSIMISM IS NOT THE ANSWER

Michael Krepon

In these times of proliferation pessimism, it is worth recalling that the United States has successfully traversed even more dangerous nuclear passages. During the Cold War, the United States was threatened by a Soviet nuclear arsenal that included thousands of nuclear weapons on hair-trigger alert. We were engaged in a nuclear arms race that produced tens of thousands of weapons. On average, the United States or the Soviet Union tested one nuclear weapon per week, from the Cuban Missile Crisis to the fall of the Berlin wall, a constant reminder of nuclear dangers. In the formative stages of the Cold War, America's primary competitors were two nuclear-armed, megalomaniacal mass murderers, Josef Stalin and Mao Zedong.

Now we are concerned about a surprise attack by terrorists armed with nuclear weapons or "dirty" bombs. Asymmetrical warfare has replaced concerns over arms racing. In addition to "loose nukes" and nuclear terrorism, we worry most about horizontal, not vertical proliferation. The newest and most worrisome aspirants for the Bomb are Iran and North Korea. In Iran, medievalist mullahs vie for control with a younger generation of Revolutionary Guards led by a Holocaust denier. In North Korea, the globe's last Stalinist regime is led by a puerile aficionado of luxury goods who rules by paranoia and starvation, and who pays for his cognac, nuclear programs, and army by exporting counterfeit currency, hard drugs, and missiles.

Dealing with North Korea and Iran is not easy, but managing relations with the Soviet Union and "Red" China was even more challenging. As worrisome as Kim Jong Il and Mahmoud Ahmadinejad are, they are no match for Stalin and Mao. With patience, persistence, and wise policies, previous American leaders managed to

contain and reduce nuclear dangers. With better leadership, relent-
less effort, and sound strategies, today's leaders can succeed, too.

It is also worth recalling that, in the formative stages of the
Cold War, there were widespread expectations that, sooner or later,
the Bomb would again be used on the battlefield, and that human
survival would be placed at dire risk. The expectation of disaster
initially prompted an ambitious effort to ban the Bomb and place
the means of its production under international control. When this
effort failed, safety became the sturdy stepchild of terror, as Winston
Churchill predicted. Nuclear overkill and national vulnerability
became the odd guardians against another crossing of the nuclear
threshold.

There could be no comfort in such means of "protection." Our
earlier nuclear concerns could have driven us to distraction, or to
wildly unsound policies. Instead, a progression of U.S. leaders of
both political parties settled on deterrence, containment, and political engagement with dangerous regimes to reduce nuclear dangers.
Engagement included protracted negotiations that eventually produced treaties limiting and then reducing the most powerful weapons
in the world. This extended undertaking also produced surprisingly
positive results despite widespread skepticism.

Two keys to the successful reduction of nuclear dangers during
the Cold War were exceptional leadership and dogged persistence.
Both were exemplified by Paul Nitze, who offered the following sage
counsel to those who despaired of preventing mushroom clouds after
the Soviet Union joined the nuclear club: "Try to reduce the dangers
of nuclear war within the relevant future time period as best you can;
you just get depressed if you worry about the long-term future."[1]
This advice—to work the nuclear problem day by day, month by
month, and year by year—is no less relevant today, when a different
set of nuclear dangers has prompted widespread anxiety.

This chapter will take snapshots of our nuclear past to place
current concerns into a historical context. I will then assess the Bush
administration's strategic concept for reducing nuclear dangers. An
administration's central strategic concept matters greatly, because the
component parts of a strategy to reduce nuclear dangers need to be
coherent, to be properly prioritized, and to engender national and
international support. If the central strategic concept of dealing with
nuclear dangers is misconceived, the mix of supporting strategies will

be deficient. Prioritization matters because the problems of nuclear proliferation and terrorism are so multifaceted that multiple, overlapping initiatives are required, and they will not always be in alignment.

A different set of difficulties can befall an administration that does not clarify a central strategic concept to reduce nuclear dangers. When this occurs, executive branch policies are more likely to become ad hoc, more susceptible to external events, and harder to defend against domestic criticism and false interpretation. The Clinton administration, which inherited a challenging, new nuclear environment, accomplished much in its first term, particularly in giving traction to efforts to secure the nuclear holdings of the former Soviet Union and to convince newly independent states on Russia's periphery to give up their sudden inheritance of nuclear weapons. But President Bill Clinton never defined and articulated a strategic concept for these efforts, and his administration progressively lost control of the nuclear agenda.

George W. Bush, unlike his predecessor, has offered a central strategic concept to reduce nuclear dangers, which I will assess, along with strategies that have been implemented to advance this concept. This chapter will conclude by highlighting areas of progress and shortfalls in the Bush administration's nuclear agenda. I also will assess the benefits and shortfalls of a traditional arms control agenda. This chapter will end with a suggested strategic concept to guide the next stage of our nuclear future. I shall highlight key elements of a new strategic concept worthy of accentuation as well as those that might best be deemphasized or jettisoned.

YEARS OF LIVING DANGEROUSLY

There have been four particularly horrific years of living dangerously in the nuclear age. The first was 1945, when the Bomb made its spectacular appearance. To many, the Bomb's threat to civilization required radical solutions, including a well-functioning world government, the abolishment of war, and international control over atomic energy. But radical solutions were not possible, so national leaders undertook a long, hard slog to prevent a third use of nuclear weapons on the battlefield. Partial solutions and incremental effort proved to be effective counters to nuclear dangers.

The second year of living dangerously was 1949, when the Soviet Union tested its first atomic bomb, President Truman endorsed a crash program to proceed with far more powerful thermonuclear (hydrogen) bombs, and the prolonged Korean War began. It was an open question whether or not atomic bombs would again be used to end another land war in Asia that at times went very badly for the United States before it ground into a bitter stalemate. The editors of the *Bulletin of the Atomic Scientists,* created by veterans of the Manhattan Project who felt remorse over their handiwork, created a clock to symbolize nuclear danger. During 1949, the minute hand of the clock stood at three minutes to midnight, the doomsday hour. Presidents Truman and Eisenhower considered preemptive attacks against new nuclear threats that followed, but rejected them as unfeasible or unwise.

The third year of living dangerously was, of course, in 1962, when the Cuban Missile Crisis played out over thirteen days. This crisis occurred before the era of communication satellites or "hotlines"—it took half a day to code, transmit (via Western Union), and translate Nikita Khrushchev's first letter to President Kennedy. In the meantime, dramas played out in a matter of minutes that could have changed the course of our nuclear history, including the debate among three officers on a Soviet submarine on whether to disobey orders and to fire a nuclear weapon while being depth-charged to the surface; the shooting down of an American U-2 spy plane over Cuba; and the most ill-timed training exercise ever, when the Air Force tested an intercontinental ballistic missile carrying a dummy warhead over the Pacific. The *Bulletin of the Atomic Scientists'* clock registered seven minutes to midnight in 1962—a generous call.

The fourth year of living dangerously was in 1983. This was the year that President Ronald Reagan declared that the Soviet Union was the focus of evil in the world, when he surprised nearly everyone by announcing the Strategic Defense Initiative to provide an Astrodome-like protection against missile attack, when Soviet air defense forces shot down a Korean Airlines jet that had strayed hopelessly off course, when the United States began to deploy "Euro-missiles," and when the Kremlin walked out of nuclear negotiations. Reagan and the Kremlin's leader, the dialysis machine-tethered former KGB chief, Yuri Andropov, each believed that trend lines were deeply adverse. Key advisers of both leaders worried about a "bolt out of the blue" nuclear attack.

Matters reached a boiling point in late 1983, when an intense Kremlin muscle-flexing campaign failed to stop the deployment of Euro-missiles that could fly so fast and so stealthily that they could not be detected in time for the Kremlin to react. Their likely targets were the nerve centers of the Soviet command and control system. For once, the United States had trumped the Soviet "machine-building" factories that pumped out missiles: NATO's rejoinder to Russian Euro-missile deployments, in the view of the Soviet defense establishment's most paranoid denizens, might just constitute the first wave of a nuclear attack that could leave the Kremlin deaf, dumb, and blind. At the very time when some in the Reagan administration were convinced that the Soviet Union had achieved and would exploit its strategic superiority, the Kremlin's intelligence apparatus was checking on U.S. blood banks and how many lights were on late at night in the Pentagon and State Department, searching for clues of an impending surprise attack.

FAST FORWARD

Compared to these harrowing years, our present dilemmas do not seem so grave or so insurmountable. Nonetheless, public anxieties are very high, stoked by unremitting threat assessments by both the Bush administration and its severest critics. Heightened threat assessments were also a staple of the Cold War, but contemporary nuclear threats have a different, more pervasive feel. The Soviet nuclear threat was more quantifiable and geographically contained. Active diplomatic engagement and nuclear negotiations provided a sense of assurance that national leaders were reducing threats. Critics of hard-line policies also had a leavening effect, offering far less harsh threat assessments. Moreover, the threat was most often framed and understood as a contest between two military establishments, not between the American and Soviet people.

After the September 11 attacks against emblematic targets on U.S. soil, threat assessments soared. Our list of adversaries extended beyond states to shadowy groups and alienated freelancers who lived far away from ancestral homes, or who found safe haven among coreligionists. Warfare was no longer confined to men and women in uniform; innocent bystanders were now prime targets. The visceral, optical "profile" of a terrorist could be met by someone in your neighborhood, on your bus or airplane. Key elements to deal with the Soviet nuclear threat, particularly nuclear overkill and national vulnerability, made absolutely no sense against the threats of "loose nukes" and nuclear terrorism. Strategies that were dismissed against old adversaries, especially preemption, were revived in the wake of attacks on the U.S. homeland during a period of unparalleled American military superiority. The focus on preemption, unlike containment, compounded public anxieties.

THE GEORGE W. BUSH ADMINISTRATION

The Bush administration's central strategic concept to reduce nuclear dangers was well-suited to these anxious times. Simply put, the Bush strategic concept was to use U.S. military, political, and economic dominance to keep Americans safe. The traumatic events of September 11 constituted a wake-up call about nuclear terrorism, loose nukes, and poorly controlled fissile material. America could wait to be struck again, or adopt proactive strategies to prevent another September 11. The Bush administration's answer to this binary choice became abundantly clear.

The foundation of a compelling strategic concept rests on a succinct definition of the problem, which the Bush administration correctly characterized as the most deadly weapons in the most dangerous hands. The "War on Terror" was born, as ambitious as the scope of the problem it sought to defeat. This label was well chosen to galvanize domestic political support and to quiet dissenters, but poorly chosen to succeed with the problem at hand. Waging war on a symptom is different than waging war on an enemy. If taken seriously, the War on Terror would be endless, and if assessed honestly, would be as likely to produce victory as, say, a war on global poverty. Great simplifiers and fearmongers unhelpfully translated the War on Terror as a war on Islam, thereby exacerbating the problem and alienating potential allies who could offer the most assistance.

The Bush administration's response to this danger was perfectly captured in its *National Security Strategy of the United States of America,* issued one year after the September 11 attacks. The document fused extraordinary American power projection with a missionary zeal to prevent the most dangerous weapons from falling into the most dangerous hands. U.S. military dominance and coalitions of the willing would be employed to "act against such emerging threats before they are fully formed. . . . History will judge harshly those who saw this coming danger but failed to act."

A freedom agenda would be pursued in parallel with the counter-proliferation and counter-terrorism agendas: "We will defend the peace by fighting terrorists and tyrants. We will preserve the peace by building good relations among the great powers. We will extend the peace by encouraging free and open societies on every continent."[2] The battle with Islamic extremism was joined.

The key elements of the new national security strategy were soon evident. New global norms to prevent nuclear terrorism would be identified, but building new international institutions and bureaucracies would be avoided. Existing global norms dealing with proliferation would be treated in a new fashion. Not all states with nuclear weapons were to be treated equally. The Bomb was no longer the problem, per se; instead, it was the character of the bomb holder that mattered. Responsible, friendly nations, such as India, should not be penalized for past deeds and, by inference, for future actions. The essence of the problem was, after all, the most dangerous weapons in the most dangerous hands.

George W. Bush's strategic concept for preventing new nuclear dangers relied primarily on U.S. military dominance to check and, if need be, nullify hostile nuclear programs and transactions. U.S. freedom of action would be a paramount objective. A war without boundaries would now be taken to the enemy; preemptive strikes and preventive wars were preferable to waiting to take another hit. Global norms that constrained others would be welcomed; those that pinched U.S. military options would be opposed. Existing treaties that served these ends would be supported. Old treaties or new ones that did not would be treated dismissively.

The Bush administration's track record in actually reducing nuclear dangers has been decidedly mixed. Admittedly, the administration has had to operate under extremely difficult circumstances. The Bomb has become an equalizer for states that feel particularly threatened by U.S. power projection capabilities. Moreover, the scope of the problem facing the Bush administration had expanded greatly, to include shadowy groups not subject to the traditional dictates of deterrence, entrepreneurial middlemen, and such radiological materials as cobalt-60, which is used in countless hospitals for cancer treatments but also could be used for "dirty" bombs.

Regrettably, the Bush administration's response to the September 11 attacks made difficult proliferation problems far worse. When a dominant power launches an unprovoked war—what American commentators have called a "war of choice"—ties with allies and other major powers will become strained. When a supposedly preventive war is fought on the basis of false assumptions and faulty intelligence, negative proliferation consequences are compounded.

Cohesion among major powers, one precondition of effective international efforts to prevent proliferation, was badly strained after the second Iraq war was joined. The two countries that felt most in need of a deterrent to prevent subsequent wars of choice—North Korea and Iran—accelerated their nuclear activities. Because U.S. intelligence was so wrong and U.S. diplomacy so unpersuasive prior to the second Iraq war, the Bush administration was poorly positioned to lead diplomatic efforts to stop and reverse the North Korean and Iranian nuclear programs. Beijing engaged in the heavy lifting required for North Korea, and there was no subsequent engagement strategy for Iran.

The Bush administration's prioritization of key elements to tackle proliferation problems also made difficult proliferation problems worse. Bush's emphasis on coercive instruments to prevent proliferation would have been far less objectionable (if not more successful) had his administration also championed treaty regimes and nonproliferation diplomacy. Instead, it disdained both. During George W. Bush's first term, his administration barely talked to North Korea and kept Iran at arm's length. The Bush team was keenly interested in stopping these "evil-doers" from acquiring the Bomb, but quite uninterested in ratifying a treaty that foreclosed U.S. nuclear testing. The administration demanded that bad actors adhere to their obligations under the Nuclear Non-Proliferation Treaty (NPT), while dismissing prior U.S. commitments to specific steps to strengthen it. The Bush team blocked multilateral treaty negotiations dealing with proliferation for four full years after the start of major combat operations in Iraq. The possibility of starting negotiations on a fissile material "cutoff" treaty opened up in 2007 at the Conference on Disarmament only after the administration withdrew its veto on discussions of space security.

The proliferation picture during the Bush administration was not unreservedly bleak, however. On the positive side of the ledger, Libya voluntarily forswore its programs to develop weapons of mass destruction, handed over its acquisitions, and allowed foreign inspectors to visit previously sensitive sites. Muamar Qadafi rightly concluded that Libya's oil was more valuable than a nuclear deterrent that might never have been assembled from crates. Qadafi exchanged his crates for foreign direct investment.

The Bush administration also made lasting contributions by emphasizing the utility of codes of conduct in combating proliferation. The administration's preferred codes took the form of political agreements among like-minded states to engage in activities designed to prevent dangerous activities. President Bush launched the Proliferation Security Initiative in May 2003 with the declared goal of seizing weapons of mass destruction or their components when in transit. A core group of eleven states agreed to a statement of interdiction principles four months later. The core group then invited other nations to associate themselves, in varying degrees of attachment, to these principles.

The administration also supported the Hague Code of Conduct to supplement the Missile Technologies Control Regime. Most countries—with the notable exceptions of China, Pakistan, India, North Korea, Syria, and Iran—pledged to prevent the proliferation of ballistic missiles capable of carrying weapons of mass destruction and to exercise restraint in ballistic missile testing and development.

Another important nonproliferation initiative championed by the Bush administration was United Nations Security Council Resolution 1540, unanimously approved in April 2004, imposing binding obligations on all member states "to take additional effective measures to prevent the proliferation of nuclear, chemical or biological weapons and their means of delivery." This resolution calls on all nations to establish effective domestic controls, including criminal statutes, to prevent proliferation.

In addition, the Bush administration has taken steps to increase the financing and geographical scope of cooperative threat reduction efforts. In June 2002, the United States and its G-8 partners announced the Global Partnership Against the Spread of Weapons and Materials of Mass Destruction. In July 2006, President Bush and Russian president Vladimir Putin announced a Global Initiative to Combat Nuclear Terrorism that focused on improved material protection, control, and accounting; increased cooperation for detecting and suppressing illicit trafficking; and enhanced consequence management.

Ambition has far exceeded reach, and implementation has been slow and spotty for these initiatives. But the same could be said for the Nonproliferation Treaty itself, which required great effort to secure broader participation and improved implementation. The Bush administration deserves credit for championing these initiatives. Over time, and with comparable effort, they, too, will gain broader participation and better implementation.

Despite these positive steps, on balance, the Bush administration has left much repair work for its successor. The negative consequences of Iraq—the first war of choice to prevent proliferation—have overshadowed the administration's positive contributions. Moreover, the Bush administration's positive accomplishments were quite explicitly fashioned as alternatives to new multilateral treaties, for which it had considerable disdain. The global nonproliferation system is based on norms that are embedded in treaties, most importantly the Nonproliferation Treaty. "Regime keeping" therefore depends on the continued nurturing and strengthening of international agreements that necessarily constrain U.S. nuclear options as well as those of potential adversaries.

The administration's highly selective approach to nonproliferation—supporting obligations that constrain others while sloughing off those that constrain the nuclear options of America or its friends—has done considerable harm. Supplementary arrangements can usefully reaffirm, but not substitute for, core treaty obligations. The bedrock commitments on which international support for the Nonproliferation Treaty is built include nuclear disarmament, an end to nuclear testing, and the stoppage of fissile material production for nuclear weapons. This global nonproliferation system could have been constructed and sustained only if these norms applied to all. It can be harmed only by adopting one set of rules that apply to "good guys" and another for bad actors. The Bush administration's damaging innovation of a "good versus bad" template for proliferation has done more harm than good, and is worth jettisoning.

Is Arms Control Still Relevant?

Arms control came into vogue in the early 1960s, at just the right time. The United States and the Soviet Union were paying lip service to empty slogans about "general and complete disarmament" while they were simultaneously engaged in an unprecedented, massive arms race. There was no serious communication between the contestants, no rules, and no prospects for containing the competition. The conceptualization of arms control came out of academia and think tanks and was embraced by the Kennedy administration, which hired several key proponents.

The idea of arms control was rooted in the Cold War and in a bipolar international system. It was based on the simple, yet controversial, assumption that even the most intense ideological and geopolitical competition could have a zone of common interest, and within that zone, rules, tacit and explicit, could be honored. The common interest was defined as avoiding a nuclear war. The superpower competition would naturally result in large nuclear arsenals that could be used to deter war from occurring. The primary challenge here would be to place limits on the offensive competition to prevent worst cases from being realized.

The second challenge of arms control, which was far more radical and counterintuitive, was to foreclose effective national defenses so that nuclear overkill could help keep the peace. National vulnerability was required, in the tenets of arms control, to prevent even more offensive firepower, to facilitate nuclear arms reduction, and to reaffirm in the minds of national leaders the senselessness of the nuclear war-fighting plans that were kept in locked safes. Given the stakes involved, as well as the levels of mistrust, the centerpieces of arms control needed to be formalized in legally binding treaties.

The end of the Cold War and the demise of the Soviet Union displaced the centrality of arms control and made its core characteristics of nuclear overkill and national vulnerability dangerous as well as irrelevant. In the post–Cold War world of power imbalances, asymmetric warfare replaced arms races as the central policy concern. Missile defenses made sense against worst cases and as a means of reassurance for allies threatened with proliferation, thereby serving as a brake against even more proliferation.

Old arms control arguments—pro and con—lost their audiences the more the Cold War receded into history. After six decades of non-use of nuclear weapons, the contention that a new or refurbished weapon design would somehow make it easier for national leaders to cross the nuclear threshold makes little sense. As the only nation that has used nuclear weapons in war, and as the nation with the most powerful conventional forces, the United States would lose more than it gains by initiating the use of nuclear weapons and gains more than it loses by reducing the salience of nuclear weapons.

While the audience has left the theater, new arms control rhetoricians continue to echo the past. The latest argument relates to the proposed "reliable replacement warhead." As now conceived, this program would begin by swapping out one Cold War design for a more forgiving design that would carry out much the same missions as the replaced weapon but would be easier to maintain and would presumably not need to be tested. This high-profile replacement program, unlike the current warhead refurbishment efforts undertaken by nuclear laboratories, is likely to highlight questions about why warheads designed for Cold War–era missions should be replaced at all, or how such an expensive undertaking supports the fundamental U.S. national interest of reducing the shadow cast by nuclear weapons.

Reliable replacement warhead programs can be justified only if they are one piece on a larger chessboard in which the United States reduces the salience of nuclear weapons and reaffirms the global nonproliferation system. At a minimum, high-profile and expensive reliable replacement warhead programs would need to be accompanied by U.S. ratification of the Comprehensive Test Ban Treaty and far deeper cuts in nuclear arsenals.

Even so, rationales for reliable replacement warheads are unlikely to be plausible if they rest on the need either to execute war plans reminiscent of the Cold War, or to initiate nuclear strikes against third world targets in the Bush administration's War on Terror. The key question for the United States remains, whether for Cold War designs or reliable replacements: What actual purpose, beyond generalized notions of deterrence, do nuclear weapons serve? If there is no compelling answer to this question other than generalized notions of deterrence, then the design of replacement warheads could become so rudimentary, and the accompanying diplomatic initiatives so meaningful, that a replacement program could ironically serve to advance the objectives of those who are most adamantly opposed to it.

Another key tenet of arms control that took a beating after the Cold War ended was the assumption that nuclear and conventional capabilities needed to be strictly segregated. In the old days, this strengthened superpower controls against the unauthorized use of nuclear weapons while decreasing the probability, however marginal, that the nuclear threshold would be crossed in the event of hostilities. Today, the likelihood of conventional warfare between Moscow and Washington is very low, and the salience of nuclear weapons in the thinking of senior U.S. military officers has been greatly reduced by giving the Strategic Command long-range, conventional strike capabilities. Nothing clarifies the utility of conventional strike options and the disutility of nuclear strike options better than having both under one command.

Arms controllers lost many of their arguments and much of their audience after the Cold War ended. This was unavoidable, partly because any conceptualization that was designed to deal with the nuclear fears of the 1960s would not be compelling a half-century later. The decline of arms control also was accentuated because the arguments of its champions no longer resonated as new threats became increasingly evident. After the Cold War ended, opponents used the label "arms control" as a term of derision, while the media continued to designate critics of nuclear weapons development as "arms controllers."

This reflexive labeling is unhelpful for many reasons, especially because it perpetuates tired arguments and old ways of thinking. It also unfairly dismisses the entire arms control canon, much of which remains essential in preventing new nuclear dangers. The normative-based system necessary for this work was built upon arms control treaties. Treaties forged between superpowers during the Cold War may have lost part of their rationale, but they still provide necessary underpinning to global control regimes such as the Nonproliferation Treaty, which depends, in part, upon steady reductions in existing nuclear arsenals to keep the allegiance of the many non-nuclear states. Existing treaties also affirm the cooperative relations between major powers that are a precondition for successful efforts to reduce new nuclear threats.

Intrusive on-site inspections became accepted, after decades of tireless effort in the face of Cold War paranoias, as an integral feature of arms treaty regimes. It would be senseless to dispense with these verification arrangements on the grounds that the Cold War is over. After all, some of the unfinished business of Cold War arms control—particularly treaties banning nuclear tests and fissile material production for weapons—remains essential for a norms-based system to prevent new nuclear threats. As long as critics continue to insist that arms control constitutes a "Cold War"—and thus implicitly obsolete—agenda, and as long as those with whom they lock horns continue to describe themselves as arms controllers, we will waste time and energy in tired arguments rather than in building new barriers to proliferation and nuclear terrorism.

A Strategic Concept and Best Practices for Trying Times

The nature of the proliferation and terrorism challenges we face is so complex that many different initiatives will be required to tackle them. The strategic concept we choose for these challenges will be built upon diplomatic engagement, deterrence, containment, sanctions, conventional military power, and the wide array of "cooperative threat reduction" programs that have been used to lock down dangerous weapons and materials in many countries. One other tool—preventive war—is not well-suited to the nuclear dangers we face. It belongs in the tool box, but the Bush administration has taught us costly lessons by reaching for this tool against Saddam Hussein. These challenges have been compounded because the Bush administration's central strategic concept—leadership by dominance—has generated more international resistance than support. Leadership that does not produce followers can hardly be considered an effective strategic concept.

That's the bad news. The good news is that other tools we need remain in the toolbox, and can be better utilized. New leaders and a new strategic concept that draws on best practices and deemphasizes or jettisons counterproductive practices can help the United States to rebound—just as we did during rough stretches of the Cold War.

My suggested strategic concept for reducing, preventing, and eliminating nuclear dangers is the rather prosaic one of *comprehensive threat reduction*. This term is proposed for several reasons. First, comprehensive threat reduction acknowledges the scope and complexity of the problem, as well as the breadth of the response, that is required. Second, comprehensive threat reduction lends itself to far more collaborative efforts than a strategic concept based on U.S. dominance. A comprehensive threat reduction strategy places renewed emphasis on diplomatic engagement.

Third, a comprehensive threat reduction strategy embraces a balanced approach to nonproliferation and counter-proliferation initiatives. Nonproliferation efforts cannot produce lasting success without sustained commitment to legally based norms, which requires, in turn, a recommitment to ratified treaties. Today this can be accomplished by extending and making more comprehensive the bilateral U.S.-Russian agreement on deep cuts in strategic forces, removing from limbo the treaty banning all nuclear testing, and tackling the challenges of negotiating a verifiable fissile material production ban for weapons. All of these treaties have their roots in the superpower antagonisms of the Cold War. All remain equally essential for international cooperation against today's nuclear dangers. Existing monitoring provisions need to be retained and extended to become *global* norms.

Counter-proliferation initiatives reflect the need for collaborative or, if necessary, unilateral efforts to prevent the most dangerous weapons and materials from falling into the most dangerous hands. The cornerstones of the global nonproliferation system are treaties; the cornerstones of counter-proliferation measures are "coalitions of the willing" that band together to reinforce, not substitute for, treaties. The Bush administration placed far less emphasis on the former than the latter, which lent credence to the view that its coalitions of the willing were substitutes for the treaties it held in low regard.

Counter-proliferation initiatives work best when they complement and reinforce international norms grounded in treaties. When counter-proliferation initiatives become substitutes for treaties, they become suspect. Superior U.S. military capabilities will, of course, remain available for use, if needed. But it now should be apparent that the resort to preemptive strikes and preventive war is likely to generate more proliferation than prevention.

Prevention is the key. That is why a comprehensive threat reduction strategy will rely heavily on cooperative threat reduction practices. A myriad of U.S. governmental initiatives have evolved from what originally was known as the Cooperative Threat Reduction (or the Nunn-Lugar Program)—the most important congressional initiative ever devised to reduce nuclear dangers. These programs now have a much-expanded geographical scope and far more international support.

Cooperative threat reduction has an impressive track record. Through cooperative threat reduction initiatives, we have helped to consolidate dangerous stockpiles. We have provided greatly improved security around the perimeters of sensitive sites and inside particular buildings. We have offered best practices to help other nations improve personnel reliability programs to guard against "insider threats." We have removed dangerous materials from poorly secured sites. We have provided assistance for improved transportation security, and we have observed the dismantlement of missile launchers, submarines, and bombers that once carried thousands of nuclear weapons. Our success in implementing cooperative threat reduction programs is not limited by a lack of skill, but by mistrust and the lack of resources.

Cooperative threat reduction initiatives are very much a reflection of the new world of nuclear dangers arising after the demise of the Soviet Union. The initiatives devised to deal with poorly secured nuclear weapons and materials in the former Soviet Union have been wisely adapted to deal with the possibility of nuclear terrorism. Their pace of implementation has been slower than we would like, and proper implementation has faced maddening bureaucratic and political hurdles in Russia. But far more difficult problems have been surmounted during our nuclear past. Much work remains to be done, but we know how to be successful.

Arms control was a product of the Cold War. Cooperative threat reduction is a product of our times. Cooperative threat reduction initiatives build on the successes of arms control—their intrusive activities were made possible by the precedents set for on-site inspections in Cold War–era treaties. Treaties remain important for solidifying global norms; cooperative threat reduction programs reinforce those norms in flexible, creative ways. Treaties and cooperative threat reduction programs complement each other the way that balanced

nonproliferation and counter-proliferation initiatives should complement each other. Because the breadth of contemporary nuclear dangers is potentially so great, cooperative threat reduction programs
offer the greatest return on near-term investment. None of the tools
in our tool kit have more flexibility and adaptability. Cooperative
threat reduction programs are deservedly the centerpiece of a comprehensive threat reduction strategy.

5.

TIME FOR COMPREHENSIVE POLICIES ON NUCLEAR AND BIOLOGICAL WEAPONS

Christopher F. Chyba

The United States needs comprehensive policies for its approach to nuclear, chemical, and biological weapons—so-called weapons of mass destruction (WMD).[1] The existence of these weapons presents a wide range of risks that must be managed, and decisions made in responding to them sometimes trade off against one another. A comprehensive policy is needed to recognize and evaluate these tradeoffs. [2] This chapter sketches comprehensive policies for the nuclear and biological weapons cases, the two categories of weapons most capable of causing mass civilian casualties.

It is in the realm of nuclear weapons where the absence of a comprehensive policy is most apparent, for quite practical reasons. Congress must now make decisions about funding for initiatives such as the so-called Reliable Replacement Warhead (RRW), or about the transformation of the Department of Energy's nuclear weapons complex, and what that complex should look like in 2030. How many fission cores, or "pits," for nuclear weapons will the United States need to be able to manufacture annually two decades from now? Without an understanding of U.S. goals and intentions with respect to nuclear weapons and their role in national and international security, it is hard to see how decisions such as these can be made well. [3]

PAST U.S. NUCLEAR WEAPONS POLICY

During the Cold War, the United States ultimately came to rely on a policy of deterrence (by the threat of punishment) of the Soviet

Union and then China. But this was a policy that was reached after other approaches either failed or were rejected.[4]

It remained clear during the Cold War that neither national missile defense nor civil defense could shield the U.S. population from a major Soviet missile attack. Working with the Soviets and others, the U.S. also pursued nuclear nonproliferation, anchored by the Nuclear Nonproliferation Treaty (NPT), to try to minimize the number of new nuclear powers with which it would have to contend. The NPT, and the broader nonproliferation regime surrounding it, was set in the context of a series of bilateral arms control agreements between the United States and the Soviet Union that helped to manage their bilateral nuclear relationship.

Nevertheless, nuclear deterrence was central. This policy was to some extent a choice made by the United States, given its rejection of preventive war against the nuclear programs of the Soviet Union and then China, and the overwhelming difficulties facing any defensive strategy.[5]

We are now approaching twenty years since the end of the Cold War. The Bush administration's approach has been skeptical of the applicability of much that was settled on during that time. In particular, four pillars seem central to the administration's different thinking:

- *first*, it has had a deep skepticism toward multilateral agreements and diplomacy in general, and arms control agreements in particular; and
- *second*, it has been skeptical of the utility of deterrence, not only against terrorist groups, but also with respect to certain so-called rogue regimes.

In part as a result of these first two pillars, the administration has

- *third*, placed higher hopes on *dissuasion* than was the case in the past;[6] and
- *fourth*, moved *preventive war* to a central position in U.S. thinking about and response to new threats.[7]

But the limits of this emphasis on dissuasion and preventive war are shown both in Iraq and in the expansion of Iranian and

North Korean nuclear weapons–related capabilities over the past six years—and in the understandable reluctance of the Bush administration to engage in preventive war to stop either the Iranian or North Korean programs. Preventive war comes with high costs of many types. There are only so many wars of counter-proliferation that the United States will be willing to fight.

This in turn emphasizes the need for a stronger commitment to the nuclear nonproliferation regime than is currently evident in U.S. nuclear weapons policy. So too must U.S. policy address a set of other important nuclear risks.

Nuclear Risks

At a minimum, the risks that U.S. nuclear weapons policy must now confront include the following:

- *first*, dangers left over from the Cold War, including the evolving nuclear arsenals of the P-5 (Russia's and China's, in particular), and accompanying those, the chance of mistaken launch;
- *second*, the arsenals of the nuclear powers outside the nuclear nonproliferation treaty (NPT) regime: India, Israel, Pakistan, and now North Korea;
- *third*, further nuclear proliferation, including the role of nuclear proliferation networks, as well as the ability of states within the NPT nonetheless to build up to the brink of nuclear weapons— and the pressure this may put on regional rivals with respect to their own nuclear intentions;
- *fourth*, the evolution and spread of technology relevant to nuclear weapons, for example, in particular, the spread of gas centrifuge technology;
- *fifth*, nuclear theft and smuggling; and finally,
- *sixth*, the way that all these factors interact and relate to the threat of nuclear terrorism.

All of these risks must be addressed, in an interrelated way, by U.S. nuclear weapons policy. The United States has a long-standing set of policy tools to do so, but the balance among these tools needs to be different in the coming decades than it was during the Cold War, or for that matter, than it has been for the past six years.

In particular, the United States must rethink the interactions and changing balance among strategies of dissuasion, deterrence, defense, preemptive attack, preventive war, diplomacy, and the nonproliferation regime.

A Comprehensive Nuclear Weapons Policy

What would a comprehensive nuclear weapons policy look like? The broad contours of such a policy must take into account both short-term and long-range goals.[8]

The United States must continue to strengthen the security of nuclear weapons and materials worldwide, and accelerate this process when possible. This involves cooperative threat reduction as well as the G-8 "global cleanout" efforts for removing highly enriched uranium (HEU) from around the world. It also involves the success or failure of UN Security Council Resolution 1540, a resolution that requires all nations to put in place effective domestic and export control regulations.

The United States and other members of the nonproliferation regime also should continue to take steps to tighten supply-side measures under the nonproliferation regime—the Additional Protocol of the International Atomic Energy Agency (IAEA), tightened export controls under Resolution 1540, the Proliferation Security Initiative (PSI), and other steps. The IAEA must have a budget sufficient to perform its many important monitoring and inspection duties. A well-funded, competent, respected, and independent IAEA is strongly in the enlightened self-interest of the United States.

Eliminating the North Korean nuclear weapons program and preventing Iran from achieving nuclear weapons are obvious specific nonproliferation objectives that remain critical to the health of the global nonproliferation regime, and to international security.

But it must also be recognized that in the long run, with respect to the nearly fifty states that are nuclear capable[9] and others that might try to become so, nonproliferation success depends on the demand-side drivers for nuclear weapons. In one sense, supply-side steps provide time during which demand-side pressures for nuclear weapons can be addressed. The United States needs to use that time, and it also needs to consider what factors influence the demand for nuclear weapons—including the role that its own actions may play.

To that end, the United States should work to reduce the salience of nuclear weapons in foreign affairs. To achieve this, the United States should:

- *First*, show discipline in its discussions of U.S. nuclear weapons policy. With such big sticks as its conventional dominance and the implicit threat within nuclear deterrence, the United States can afford to speak more softly in public and in policy documents with respect to potential nuclear use.
- *Second*, the United States should affirm that the mission of nuclear weapons is core deterrence—that is, the deterrence of attack using nuclear weapons against the United States or its allies.
- *Third*, the United States should reaffirm central past nonproliferation commitments. In particular, the RRW must not be allowed to lead to new nuclear testing for the purpose of verifying the reliability of a new warhead design, and the United States should reaffirm its commitment to the Comprehensive Test Ban Treaty (CTBT).

It is not clear that the RRW needs to be pursued at this time, given the reliability of the existing arsenal. But if the United States decides nevertheless to go ahead with the RRW—a warhead that is being promoted for its reliability in the absence of further nuclear testing—this should be coupled to ratification of the CTBT.

Similarly, a verifiable Fissile Material Cutoff Treaty (FMCT) should be pursued. Commitments to the CTBT and the FMCT were made by the nuclear weapon states as part of the bargain in 1995 that achieved the permanent extension of the NPT; the United States should make this visible effort to live up to its end of that bargain.

- *Fourth*, the United States should work to decrease the number of nuclear weapons held by all nuclear weapons states, and in particular should pursue further joint reductions of deployed warheads with Russia to follow the upcoming expirations of the Strategic Arms Reduction Treaty (START) and Moscow Treaty agreements (due to expire in 2009 and 2012, respectively). In the context of these reductions, the United States and Russia should also discuss ways to decrease the chances of mistaken launch.

THE WMD CONTINUUM

Nuclear, biological, and chemical weapons are often grouped together under the rubric "weapons of mass destruction," but this common term obscures important differences among these unconventional weapons with respect to ease of production and consequences of attack.[10] Imagine arraying these classes of weapons, together with the threat of cyberterrorism for the purposes of illustration, along a line extending from nuclear weapons at one end to cyber attacks at the other. A global monitoring and inspection regime is challenging but plausible in the nuclear case because the bottlenecks to producing nuclear weapons material (manufacturing highly enriched uranium or plutonium) are considerable and the number of facilities that need to be monitored are few (the IAEA monitors about 1,100 nuclear-related facilities).

At the cyber end of the continuum, however, with hundreds of millions of desk-top and laptop computers connected to the Internet worldwide, a monitoring and inspection regime is nearly inconceivable. Whatever way the world deals with the threat of cyberterrorism, it will not be through full-scope physical monitoring and inspection.

Chemical and biological weapons threats lie between these two extremes. The chemical case is closer to the nuclear, but even so the Organization for the Prohibition of Chemical Weapons (OPCW) currently must monitor over five thousand facilities. Chemical weapons are subject to a universal, nondiscriminatory ban (unlike the case of nuclear weapons, where the NPT allows the P-5 to have nuclear weapons for the time being) and subject to a system of inspection and verification (unlike the case of biological weapons, where the Biological and Toxin Weapons Convention [BWC] carries with it no credible compliance or verification protocol).

But the biological threat lies closer to the cyberterrorism end of the continuum than to the nuclear end. Moreover, as biotechnology continues to increase in power and spread globally, the biological challenge is looking ever more like the cyber challenge and less like the nuclear. Biotechnological power is literally exponentiating.[11] Just as the exponential increase in computing power described by Moore's Law has driven the move from small numbers of mainframe computers to vast numbers of ever-more-powerful personal machines, so the development and spread of biotechnology is making increasing power for biological manipulation available to smaller and smaller groups of the technically competent. There are no good models from Cold War arms control or nonproliferation efforts for how civilization is to cope with the challenge of a world in which groups or even individuals can modify (or create from scratch) dangerous organisms. In that sense, the challenge facing us is unprecedented.[12]

BIOLOGICAL RISKS

A comprehensive approach to countering biological risks must confront the challenge posed by the biotechnology explosion, but to be successful, it cannot dwell only on this challenge. It must take into account at least four different categories of biological threats:

- *first*, infectious disease, which currently kills about fourteen million globally every year (whereas the 2001 anthrax attacks in the United States killed five);
- *second*, illicit state-run or state-sponsored biological weapons programs;
- *third*, non-state actors, be they terrorist groups or "bio-hackers"; and
- *fourth*, inadvertent release of disease organisms by laboratory accidents.

As with the nuclear case, steps adopted to address one particular risk could interact negatively with what is needed to address others. Once again, therefore, a comprehensive policy is necessary.

Toward a Comprehensive Biological Security Policy

Biological weapons programs are intrinsically more difficult to detect than nuclear programs, and the technical threshold for biological terrorism is much lower—though still challenging. But defense is potentially far more effective in the biological case, provided that it is understood to mean improvements in disease surveillance and response (including surge capacity). Because flight travel times are often shorter than disease incubation times, for national security as well as public health reasons disease surveillance and response must be improved internationally as well as nationally. Improvements in disease surveillance and response will help reduce the burden of infectious disease due to natural causes worldwide, even in the absence of terrorist attacks. Most of the response to the international SARS outbreak in 2003 did not depend on whether that new virus was the result of a terrorist act or the product of a natural emergence of a novel virus into the human population. Either way, there was a disease epidemic that had to be defeated.

Since new diseases continue to emerge regularly into the human population—one new disease, on average, has emerged annually for the past several decades—we can be sure that there will be many more such examples in the future. For this reason alone, steps taken to secure pathogens and constrain access to them in order to curtail opportunities for bioterrorism must be sure not to interfere with the global collaborations essential to understanding and stopping outbreaks of newly emerged diseases.

Moreover, it is strongly in the self-interest of the United States to improve national and international disease surveillance and response. It is extraordinary in this context that the Global Pathogen Surveillance Act, despite having been introduced in Congress several times, has never passed. This Act would establish a program of bilateral assistance for developing countries to improve their disease surveillance and response capacity—with respect to communications, laboratory equipment, and training. Fully funding this plan would require only a small fraction of what the United States now spends annually, and not always effectively, on biodefense.

Not all steps that should be taken with respect to bioterrorism will have the dual benefit of supporting public health infrastructure regardless of whether bioterrorist attacks ever occur. Certain steps—

assuming that they can be pursued competently—should continue to be targeted toward particular organisms, such as the anthrax bacterium and the smallpox virus. But the pace of advances in biotechnology also means that there will be an ever-expanding threat spectrum that civilization could conceivably face. As with the nuclear case, it therefore remains important to understand motivational issues—and in particular, to examine the reasons why so few modern intentional biological attacks have taken place.

Exponentiating biotechnology provides an extraordinary challenge to traditional arms control and, possibly, to human civilization. A wide variety of response strategies are now being discussed, but all of them face important objections.[13] The good news is that these concerns are being recognized internationally—an essential step in finding solutions, given the globalization of the technology. In 2006, UN secretary-general Kofi Annan wrote that biological weapons were "the most important under-addressed threat relating to terrorism" and warned of the danger of "designer diseases and pathogens."[14] He subsequently called for a bottom-up approach toward finding solutions, bringing together international stakeholders to suggest ways forward.

While many analysts in the United States emphasize the threats posed by globalizing biotechnology, perspectives in the developing world may be quite different. In October 2005, an African meeting on these issues released the Kampala Compact, declaring that although "the potential devastation caused by biological weapons would be catastrophic for Africa," it is "illegitimate" to address biological weapons threats without addressing infectious disease and other key public health issues.[15] Given the global burden of disease, and the globalized nature of biotechnology, it is crucial that the developed and developing world find common ground on this issue—and the United Nations likely remains the best venue for such efforts.

Focus on the implications of the biotechnology revolution and terrorism must, in a comprehensive strategy, be moderated by the importance of not contributing to any new bioweapons arms race among states. Steps that the United States takes to address bioterrorism—especially programs that reportedly consider genetic modifications to microorganisms in order to determine the threat such creations might pose—should be subject to this kind of strategic oversight, not merely legal review to ensure formal compliance with the BWC. While efforts during the 1990s to achieve a compliance protocol to the BWC ended when the Bush administration withdrew from the negotiations in July 2001, ongoing or new efforts within the BWC framework to combat bioterrorism, to increase awareness among biologists and others of the dual-use nature of certain biological research, and to increase transparency among state programs as a way of confidence building, should be pursued.

CONCLUSION

Despite the vastly different challenges that biological and nuclear weapons pose, they are similar insofar as both involve such a wide spectrum of risks that policies adopted to address one or another specific dilemma could be counterproductive overall if they failed to take into account impacts on other parts of the threat spectrum. This is no more than a way of saying that policy-making in these areas must strive to be comprehensive, attempting to weigh overall benefits and costs. In some ways the biological case is the more daunting, because biotechnology poses a challenge to which there currently are only partial answers. But we also still live in a world where there are tens of thousands of intact nuclear warheads (an estimated 16,000 in Russia), with the prospect that more countries might try to join the club.[16] It is time for comprehensive policies to address risks in both domains. This chapter has sketched one approach. Future policy-makers will need to improve on these ideas.

6.

REMEMBERING NONPROLIFERATION PRINCIPLES

William C. Potter

O nce upon a time, in the not too distant past, it was relatively easy to identify the nonproliferation purists. They were the true believers in the Nuclear Non-Proliferation Treaty (NPT) and its associated institutions such as the International Atomic Energy Agency (IAEA). These states, which could be counted on to lead the charge in support of the treaty's core principles and to insist upon strict adherence to all of its provisions, included Australia, Canada, Germany, Ireland, Japan, New Zealand, Norway, South Africa, and Sweden. The United States and Russia also typically were leaders of the nonproliferation chorus, although they tended to sing more softly and off-key whenever the lyrics touched upon the treaty's disarmament provisions.

All of these states played crucial roles when the NPT was extended indefinitely in 1995, and also in 2000, when the NPT Review Conference endorsed important new disarmament and nonproliferation measures. In addition, a number of the countries joined together in like-minded political groupings such as the New Agenda Coalition to provide a bridge between nuclear weapon states (NWS) and non-nuclear weapon states (NNWS) on contentious disarmament and nonproliferation issues.

Today, although a few of these nonproliferation stalwarts continue to champion the cause consistently, most former members of the core group have retreated to a more selective embrace of NPT principles and practices. This posture, which was evident in the United States' stance at the 2005 NPT Review Conference, has become manifest among many other countries in the past eighteen months.

This shift toward "cherry-picking" of nonproliferation commitments is most evident with respect to the debate over extending nuclear trade to India, but it may reflect a more fundamental reevaluation on the part of many countries about the relative importance to attach to economic, political, and nonproliferation objectives.

To Trade, or Not to Trade?

At the heart of the current debate over nonproliferation priorities in many capitals is the issue of whether, and under what conditions, countries should jettison export controls and other policies that preclude civil nuclear energy cooperation and trade with countries not party to the NPT or otherwise lacking safeguards on all of their nuclear facilities (so-called comprehensive or full-scope safeguards). The precipitant for this debate was the announcement on July 18, 2005, by President George W. Bush and Prime Minister Manmohan Singh that the United States and India had reached a historic agreement to cooperate in the civilian nuclear energy sector. The announcement, which had the effect of overturning more than a quarter-century of U.S. nonproliferation declaratory policy, was made with little interagency debate and without consultations between the White House and Congress or between the United States and its allies. It also was criticized by most nonproliferation experts, a notable exception being IAEA director-general Mohamed ElBaradei. Despite strong opposition from the arms control community, the White House–driven initiative gained remarkable bipartisan support in the U.S. Congress, culminating in passage of the U.S.-India Peaceful Atomic Energy Cooperation Act by an overwhelming vote (359–68 in the House and 85–12 in the Senate).

The bill was signed into law by President Bush on December 18, 2006. Before the United States can commence nuclear trade with India, however, (a) the two parties must negotiate a bilateral nuclear cooperation accord, (b) India must conclude a safeguards agreement with the IAEA, (c) the forty-five members of the Nuclear Suppliers Group (NSG) must reach consensus on an exception for India to standard guidelines governing nuclear exports, and (d) Congress must approve the bilateral nuclear agreement.

It is not the purpose of this essay to assess the overall merits of the U.S.-India nuclear deal. The extended and convoluted process by which the U.S. Congress has moved to revise domestic law to accommodate nuclear commerce with India has been the subject of much scholarly analysis and media commentary.[1] Considerable media attention—at least in nuclear trade publications—also has been given to plotting the twists and turns of the ongoing deliberations by the NSG over a U.S.-initiated proposal to create a special exception for India to the NSG's standard export control guidelines. This proposal, which requires consensus in order to be adopted, has been hotly debated at meetings of the NSG, most recently at a Consultative Group session in April 2007 in Cape Town, South Africa. At the time of this writing, it appears as though no consensus has yet been reached, although most NSG members are inclined to subordinate nonproliferation considerations to those of economic and political interests and at least tacitly support the proposed exception to the guidelines.

Surprisingly, the debate over nuclear trade with India to date has largely ignored a core nonproliferation issue—whether nuclear trade with a non-NPT party and without full-scope safeguards is compatible with existing NPT political commitments. Even more noteworthy by its absence in the debate is the issue of how states plan to reconcile their legal obligations under nuclear-weapon-free zones (NWFZs) with expression of intent to engage in commerce prohibited by zonal treaties. It is almost as if states with these obligations are unaware of them.

THE STRENGTH OF POLITICAL COMMITMENTS TO NPT PRINCIPLES AND OBJECTIVES

The process by which the NPT was extended indefinitely in 1995 was a complex one, and the result was not assured until the last moment. Central to the outcome was an arrangement orchestrated by conference president Jayantha Dhanapala to link the decision about indefinite extension of the NPT to two other decisions and one resolution—a package whose general contours were suggested by South Africa, with the strong support of Canada.[2] In addition to the decision to extend the NPT indefinitely, the package included a decision on "Strengthening the Review Process for the Treaty" and on "Principles and Objectives for Nuclear Non-Proliferation and Disarmament," as well as a "Resolution on the Middle East." These very diverse elements, which were attractive to different political groupings, were essential in gaining the conference's support for the extension decision, and all of the elements together were adopted without a vote.[3]

One of the least contentious items included in the list of twenty "Principles and Objectives" was the principle (Paragraph 12) that new nuclear supply arrangements should require full-scope safeguards as a precondition of export. This approach was a logical extension of a similar guideline adopted in 1992 by the NSG. However, it is a requirement most NPT states parties today prefer to ignore when it applies to India.

It is perhaps unsurprising that the United States should engage in such selective inattention, as it has employed since at least 2004 the dubious practice of picking and choosing which elements from prior NPT review conference decisions and documents it continues to support and which it disavows because political circumstances have changed. What is more striking is that so many critics of U.S. "cherry-picking" should adopt precisely the same practice when it comes to the inconvenient Paragraph 12 that constrains nuclear commerce with India. This indictment applies with special force to South Africa and Canada, which are widely viewed as the key architects and watchdogs of the 1995 NPT package.

THE FORCE OF LEGAL OBLIGATIONS UNDER NWFZS

If there is some ambiguity about whether the 1995 NPT Review and Extension Conference decisions are legally binding, there is no uncertainty regarding the South Pacific and African NWFZs. The case is particularly clear-cut with respect to the Treaty of Rarotonga, which entered into force on December 11, 1986. Australia and New Zealand are among the thirteen full members of the treaty from the region, and also belong to the Nuclear Suppliers Group.[4] Article 4 (a)(i) of the Treaty of Rarotonga mandates parties not to provide nuclear material or equipment unless it is subject to IAEA safeguards, the comprehensive nature of which is further elaborated on in Annex 2 of the treaty dealing with "IAEA safeguards."

A similar full-scope safeguards provision is found in Article 9 of the Treaty of Pelindaba, the African NWFZ named after the site where South Africa manufactured nuclear material for its weapons program. This treaty, which was opened for signature in April 1996, has not yet entered into force. However, a large number of African states, including South Africa, already have ratified the treaty and are legally obligated to abide by its terms as specified both by national law and by the 1969 Vienna Convention on Treaties.

Notwithstanding their zonal obligations, South Africa and Australia are expected to endorse creation of a special exception for India under the NSG guidelines. This exception would allow nuclear trade even though India does not meet the regular NSG requirements regarding full-scope safeguards.

The EU as a Nonproliferation Bellwether

A number of analysts have pointed to the emergence of the European Union as a significant positive force for nonproliferation in recent years.[5] In support of this thesis, they note the common and comprehensive platform pursued by the large block of EU states at the 2005 NPT Review Conference and a similar common position to promote the entry into force of the Comprehensive Test Ban Treaty (CTBT). They also cite the innovative application of "soft power" in requiring a nonproliferation clause in new EU trade and investment agreements with other states. This standard clause includes language requiring the trading partner to take steps to sign, ratify, or accede to and fully implement international nonproliferation and disarmament treaties and agreements such as the NPT and the CTBT. More generally, the EU has emphasized the goals of "strengthening the international system of nonproliferation, pursuing universalization of multilateral agreements, and reinforcing strict implementation and compliance with these agreements."[6]

Although the nature of the European Union has precluded the use of traditional security-oriented nonproliferation tools, it has begun to apply with some success a variety of measures involving finance and trade to encourage prudent nonproliferation behavior.[7] This approach involves the strict and consistent application of the principle of conditionality—that is, linking good nonproliferation practices to access to European markets and investments. As one prominent European analyst has observed, "'hard' conditionality should ideally become a *sine qua non* of access to European aid and markets."[8]

What is needed to make soft nonproliferation power effective, according to this perspective, is the inclusion in future EU nonproliferation clauses of "specific commitments such as CTBT ratification . . . and, most importantly, ratification of the IAEA's Additional Protocol."[9] Unfortunately, precisely the opposite is now being seriously contemplated within the EU with respect to India.

According to Annalisa Giannella, the personal representative of EU high representative for nonproliferation, Javier Solana, a number of EU states are pressing for the deletion of the standard WMD nonproliferation clause in a pending trade and investment agreement with India. Giannella is reported to have argued convincingly that were the EU to adopt such a double standard it would be necessary to abandon the conditionality clause altogether in future agreements with third countries.[10]

It is uncertain, however, if a principled nonproliferation stance will prevail in view of India's strong opposition to the clause and India's lure as a huge, lucrative market for European trade and investment. A precedent for a less stringent EU stance already can be found in the December 2005 EU decision to include India in a 10 billion euro project to build an experimental nuclear fusion reactor, although EU officials have sought to downplay the nonproliferation impact of that deal.[11]

Unusual Deviation or New Norm?

It remains to be seen if subordination of nonproliferation objectives to other considerations will be a fleeting phenomenon or an enduring fact. A disturbing sign is that, in a number of capitals, the decision about nuclear trade with India appears to have been made by officials without responsibility for nonproliferation matters and with little regard for its proliferation implications. This is clearly the case in the United States and Canada, and also appears to be the case in Australia, Brazil, Germany, and Sweden, as well as in other members of the NSG.

Indeed, among the long-time nonproliferation stalwarts that are also members of the NSG, only Ireland and New Zealand have consistently objected to the special exception for India.[12] Interestingly, among the very large and diverse group of Non-Aligned Movement

(NAM) members, which traditionally emphasize disarmament over nonproliferation considerations, only Indonesia has been vocal in objecting to the double standard conveyed by nuclear trade with a non-NPT party. This position probably is not unrelated to the fact that Indonesia, unlike South Africa, is not a major nuclear exporter.[13]

At the end of April 2007, members of the NPT will convene in Vienna for a two-week negotiation to initiate the next cycle of the treaty review process. This forum, known formally as the first session of the 2010 Preparatory Committee for the 2010 NPT Review Conference, provides an excellent opportunity to test the commitment of treaty members to their political and legal obligations, and the relative priority they attach to different foreign policy objectives.

Given the barren results of the 2005 NPT Review Conference, there is a strong temptation by members to avoid contentious issues and to seek a "smooth" PrepCom outcome. Although this attitude is understandable, it also is unfortunate, since it is likely to discourage debate on the most difficult and pressing proliferation issues, including that of nuclear trade with non-NPT parties.

In particular, those states that continue to think of themselves as leaders of the nonproliferation community would do well to remember the principles that used to guide their nonproliferation policies and for which they took justifiable pride. Otherwise they may rightly be accused of adopting the expedient philosophy expressed by the American humorist Groucho Marx: "Those are my principles, and if you don't like them . . . well, I have others."

7.

RESTORING FAITH IN THE DOUBLE BARGAIN

Hans Blix

THE DOUBLE BARGAIN

My starting point is 1968, the signing of the Nuclear Non-Proliferation Treaty (NPT). The non-nuclear weapons states of the world were asked to remain non-nuclear, and the nuclear states committed themselves to negotiate nuclear disarmament. This is the double bargain that people always used to talk about, and taken together these commitments envisage a path to a nuclear-weapon-free world.

The nuclear weapons states that existed in 1968 could have had support only for a treaty that aimed, in effect, at a nuclear-weapon free world. Other states would not have gone along with the treaty if it had not included that clause. It would not have been enough simply to promise facilitating transfer of technology. Nor, in 1995, would the treaty have been prolonged without a final date if the nuclear weapons states had not at the review conference confirmed their commitment to very concrete measures of nuclear disarmament, which were further elaborated in 2000.

Today many non-nuclear weapons states feel that the failure of the nuclear weapons states to move decisively toward nuclear disarmament amounts to a breach of faith on their part. In the view of many non-nuclear states, the five NPT nuclear weapons states seem to have abandoned the effort to which they had committed. They have forsaken the effort to move toward a nuclear weapon-free world through unilateral, bilateral, and multilateral agreements, toward a common system of global rules. Instead today they aim, through their collective power, only to stop the number of nuclear weapons states at eight.

That is perceived as the present aim of the five original nuclear weapons states. And the reduction that has occurred in the number of nuclear weapons in the nuclear weapons states—from 55,000 to some 27,000—is seen mainly as doing away with a lot of redundancy that existed, not as a sincere and significant step toward nuclear disarmament.

The obligation under Article VI of the NPT for negotiations culminating in disarmament was not put there just for the sake of negotiations but to reach results. And so there is a sense among a large number—if not all—of the non-nuclear weapons states parties to the NPT that the double bargain was in fact a one-sided deal: they see that more is being asked of them even as the nuclear weapons states seem less and less sincere in holding up their end. As a result, many see the entire regime as strained to the breaking point.

TOWARD A TURNING POINT?

I do not want to dramatize the unraveling of the NPT, which has been a very successful treaty. Consider the many states parties, including those in regions fraught with tension, that have joined and refrained from nuclear armaments. Consider its role in Ukraine, Belarussia, Kazakhstan, and South Africa, which each have stepped back from nuclear arsenals. These are tremendous successes.

Moreover, of the failures, two have been remedied. The first was Iraq, where rigorous inspections in the 1990s succeeded, against the expectations of many, in disarming Saddam Hussein's WMD programs. The second is Libya, which is in the process of eliminating its WMD program and has already made great progress.

The Cold War has ended. In the view of a growing number of governments, the way to restore faith in the system that was jointly established in 1968 and reaffirmed in 1995 is for the nuclear weapons states to take the lead in significant disarmament measures. The January op-ed in the *Wall Street Journal* by Henry Kissinger, George Shultz, William Perry, and Sam Nunn is one swallow that may hopefully signal an imminent spring.[1] But it is too early, really, to be very optimistic.

In light of the events in Iraq, and also perhaps of those in Lebanon as well, there is growing public recognition, including within the United States, that using military means to tackle proliferation and terrorism has incurred horrible costs in lives and resources. There is a recognition that the time may have come for disarmament and diplomacy.

The Weapons of Mass Destruction Commission, which I chaired, offered a long list of steps that legislatures, the public, and nongovernmental organizations could call upon governments to implement early. Such a list is actually not difficult to draw up: there are some obvious needs and some obvious candidates. Among these steps is the bringing into force of the CTBT; the Fissile Material Cutoff Treaty (FMCT), which bans production of more plutonium and highly enriched uranium; the adoption of treaty-based security guarantees; the withdrawal of nuclear weapons from the center of Europe back to Russia and the United States; and so forth.

The list can be made very long, and many things can be done overnight if there were the political will to do so. Mr. Kissinger and his colleagues included a number of these steps, and while some of them may appear modest, the main thing is to turn the tide. We have not seen that yet, but perhaps there is some little hope there.

THE PROBLEM OF UNEQUAL OBLIGATIONS

There is growing dissatisfaction among non-nuclear weapons states that even while the nuclear weapons states are ignoring their own commitments to disarmament, they remain intent on tying non-nuclear weapons states to ever more commitments. The additional safeguard protocol of the IAEA, for instance, seems an obvious candidate for adoption and would strengthen nonproliferation. In 1991, when the IAEA inspectors, for whom I was at the time responsible as director-general, found that the Iraqis had been cheating, we immediately put forward a proposal for strengthening the safeguard system, and eventually got the additional protocol. But the protocol is not universally subscribed to. Building support for this measure would not have been nearly so difficult if there had not been a general clash between the two groups at the NPT Review Conference.

Now non-nuclear weapons states are being asked to renounce their right to enrich uranium and reprocess fuel. There is much discussion about the fuel cycle, and various schemes have emerged—either through inducements or through restrictions—to require non-nuclear weapons states to renounce enrichment. None of these plans so far, I think, would work with Australia or Canada or Brazil or several other states. Restrictions on enrichment are seen as yet another thing demanded of the non-nuclear weapons states.

Yet another issue that certainly deserves discussion is the question of the right to withdrawal, which is laid down in the NPT. We all talk about making it more difficult for states to leave the treaty regime; we discussed it in the WMD Commission report and said that, at the least, one could ask that a withdrawal should be discussed and considered in the UN Security Council. The Security Council has demanded that North Korea go back to the NPT. But what is that but a denial of the state's right to withdrawal? Is that coming as well? It may be welcome to some, but it is nevertheless something that effectively imposes stronger obligations on the non-nuclear weapons states. The nuclear weapons states themselves are not moving toward disarmament—why are they asking more of the other side?

So this is the impasse where we find ourselves. I think that it will be difficult to turn the tide unless there is a change of attitude among the nuclear weapons states. They should take the lead toward substantial disarmament, and the single step that would do the most good would be moving forward on a ratification of the CTBT. No other measure in the field of arms control could help more to dispel the current despair about arms control.

Continued reliance upon the current moratorium may not be sustainable. Consider the recent condemnation of North Korea for testing a weapon. Among the states that most vigorously condemn North Korea, and which have led action against it in the Security Council, are the United States and China, which themselves have not accepted the CTBT's binding prohibition on testing. In not ratifying the CTBT, they assert the freedom to test in the future, and some groups baldly advocate renewed nuclear tests. They nonetheless feel perfectly free to condemn North Korea for doing it. I regret that North Korea tested—the world is not helped by it at all—but I see the feeling of inequality under the two-tier system we have.

HOLDOUTS FOREVER?

Three states have remained steadfastly outside the NPT: Pakistan, Israel, and India. Never having joined it, they cannot be said to have committed any breach of NPT obligations. They developed nuclear weapons. And the background was security. India looked at China, Pakistan looked at India, and Israel looked at all the Arab states—and, in the 1960s, they not only looked but also fought. It was security concerns that lay behind the policy decision in each of these three holdout states to develop nuclear weapons.

While they have not breached the NPT, the results are nevertheless lamentable. Their refusal has meant an increase in the number of nuclear weapons states, an increased temptation to further proliferation among other neighbors, and an increased risk of their conflicts turning nuclear. As we look for ways to eliminate such risks, we have to ask all those who have nuclear weapons to join in—and that's not just the five enshrined in the NPT, it is these others too. We have heard the answer from India for a long time, that it is willing to go ahead with disarmament, if the initial five nuclear states take the lead—and obviously the ones with the biggest stockpiles, the United States and Russia, should take the lead. Recently Sonia Gandhi reaffirmed that India still holds to this position—that is, that they remain willing to embrace nuclear disarmament, but will look to the big weapons states to start.

Pakistan might declare, and India, too, that it would join the moratorium on testing. Perhaps they could do something even more daring. Perhaps India and Pakistan, in their newfound cooperation, could turn to the United States and to China and say, if you ratify the CTBT, we will as well.

As for Israel, we often hear from the Arab side that the first step is for Israel to join the NPT, and only after that is done might one try to get to a zone free of all weapons of mass destruction. I think that is totally unrealistic. A zone free of weapons of mass destruction is much broader and addresses Israeli security concerns—and might have a greater chance of satisfying the Israelis than just signing on the NPT dotted line today.

In the WMD Commission report we offered another idea, though this may not be an immediately realistic one. Fears about Iran have created a new dynamic, triggering Security Council insistence that

the Iranians halt enrichment. Israel, above all, is deeply and existen-
tially concerned about what could happen in the future if Islamic Iran
were to get a cache of nuclear weapons. Israelis have a great stake in
this—arguably the largest stake in a non-nuclear Iran. Perhaps Israel
could contribute to securing a renunciation or suspension of enrichment by Iran through some measure of its own. Our commission
came up with the idea of a nuclear fuel cycle–free zone. Gulf states
have announced an interest in nuclear power, and Jordan and Egypt
have said the same. Having said that they want nuclear power, will
these countries go on to say they also want to have enrichment, all
of them? No one can feel comfortable about such enrichment domi-
noes. Perhaps it is time to consider initiating a collective long-term
renunciation of the right of enrichment and reprocessing, somewhat
like North and South Korea have done.

Yes, this would mean that Israel would have to stop making more
plutonium. And yes, it would not affect the bombs they have, and
that certainly would be the Arab objection, that Israel will still be sitting on two hundred nuclear bombs. But we should ask whether this
would not be better than the way things are going now. The Israelis
would keep, at least for the time being, what they regard as life insurance—their existing arsenal—pending wider agreements on weapons
and political relations. But preventing more enrichment processing in
a region that is so sensitive is very much in everyone's interest. In a region where the confidence is so thin, maybe it would be a useful idea.

A POROUS WALL

The inequalities in the system extend beyond the NPT's Article VI
(on disarmament) and can also be observed by the attitudes of certain states—and among members of the arms control community—
toward the Article IV right to the peaceful use of nuclear energy. It is
true that an important part of the origin of the NPT was the fear that
industrialized countries such as Germany, Sweden, and Switzerland
would start by developing nuclear power but would find a porous
wall through which they would divert highly enriched uranium or
plutonium for weapons purposes. That did not happen. And in fact
when we look at which states acquired nuclear weapons, you will
find that in practically every case they were seeking weapons first

and nuclear power second. China had nuclear weapons long before it had nuclear power. Iraq went for nuclear weapons and not for nuclear power. Israel still has only nuclear weapons and no nuclear power, although it seems to be encouraged by the Indian example to seek U.S. support for a similar arrangement. Iran seems to be the concern today, and there are fears that its nuclear program may be hiding a weapon ambition.

When states have sought nuclear weapons, they have done so mostly for security reasons. It is not that they have been tempted, like naughty children, to cross from peaceful nuclear use into military use. That has been a concern, but it is not really borne out by the experience.

Nevertheless, proposals have come forward for how to remedy this perceived risk, and one is an international fuel bank that would ensure supply of nuclear fuel and thus make domestic enrichment programs uneconomic and superfluous. However, an IAEA panel tasked with how to structure such a fuel bank could not find a solution, and I do not think it is an easy puzzle to solve. The United States proposal in 2006 for a Global Nuclear Energy Partnership (GNEP) is very ingenious, but its realization lies twenty years in the future. Other options for a fuel bank seem similarly far in the future.

The central question with any fuel bank remains: Who will decide? Who will decide who can take the loan in the bank? Who can buy the fuel from the bank? Presumably participation will be voluntary, and I think some governments would contribute to it, and the prices are going to be reasonable—all well and good. But who will decide whether Venezuela can buy fuel for a research reactor or not? I think that is the big problem.

Some people argue that there is a problem with the notion of an inalienable right to access nuclear power. But this is not a question of rights under the NPT—after all, if we did not have the NPT, anyone would be free to do so. In the domestic sphere, citizens are obliged to abide by laws whether or not they agree with them, and are likely to be punished if they do not comply. States, on the other hand, may join or not join, ratify or not ratify treaties, depending on the advantages they see. Hence to attract adherence and compliance, it is important to create such conditions that states want to join.

So if you delete the NPT, everybody will be free to do as they choose. It is the NPT that says that countries assume certain restrictions voluntarily. First, countries are asked, under the NPT, to commit themselves not to develop nuclear weapons. Then they are asked to take a further step and say they will also commit themselves to no fuel cycle. And now they are also being asked to forgo nuclear power. This has, for example, been proposed in the negotiations with North Korea. Certainly the initial U.S. position was that there could be no nuclear power at all in North Korea. I do not think that the world is going to go along with that.

Critics of nuclear power underestimate the positive role that peaceful nuclear energy can play. Already it provides the world with about as much electricity as does hydropower, and it does so with practically no greenhouse gas emissions. All energy sources have problems. The continued reliance on hydrocarbons has very real implications, not only in the dangers of the greenhouse emissions but also in the dangers of the competition over oil resources, which has contributed to stress in many of the world's tensest regions, from the Middle East to Central Asia.

Admittedly, nuclear energy has its risks, but proliferation may not even be primary among them. As I have argued, states that have gone for nuclear weapons have not been tempted to cross the border from peaceful programs, but have sought weapons for security reasons. A more severe risk is posed by the issue of security in everyday operation, but this too, like the question of waste, can be managed.

Two Distinct Visions of Security

How is it that our national societies, or at least most of them, have come to peace and are not using weapons against each other all the time? In the wild history of my own Nordic countries, the clans and families were constantly fighting—in a sense you had blood revenge as a way of mutually assured deterrence. How did we escape this cycle?

John Locke has said that the criteria distinguishing a civilized society are its rules regarding third-party settlement or arbitration of disputes. Historically, in the early Middle Ages, conciliation and arbitration were used to get away from the vendettas and blood revenges. I would argue that our ability to avoid armed conflicts and become "civilized" cannot succeed unless it is rooted in similar adherence to the rule of law.

But there was another element. If another criterion of civilized society is the authorities' monopoly on the possession and use of weapons, this state can come about in several ways. Historically, the most common way in national societies was for one thug or big chief to take control of the whole thing, which gradually evolved into the king's peace. He said that anyone who disturbs the peace is acting against me, and I will take action. You give your weapons to me, and I will maintain control and give you peace. It was not a democracy, it was more a tyranny, but tyranny perhaps was better than anarchy. And eventually the use of this force and the possession of these weapons submitted to rules of society, and that has become the rule of law we want to have now.

In most countries today there is a belief that rule of law, arbitration, and conciliation comprise the path to security. Among others, including perhaps some of the philosophers in the Pentagon, there is a belief in a second model, and a sense that they should play the role of the big chief that pacifies a violent world. This is articulated in the president's national security strategy, which asserts that U.S. power will provide the possibility for not only a more peaceful but also a better world.

This view gained momentum in the United States after 1991 when Iraq's clandestine nuclear program was uncovered. The military side, in particular, felt that the multilateral system was demonstrably not working. Here was a treaty, the NPT, which was respected by the good guys but was not respected by the bad guys. Here you had an inspection system set up under the nonproliferation treaty and it did not work. The IAEA was the watchdog, but it did not see what was happening in the 1980s.

That is true, we had not seen what happened, because the system was not sufficient—but neither had the Israelis, nor the CIA, so we were in pretty good company. And this coincided, incidentally, with the end of the Cold War and the enormous increase in the relative military strength of the United States, which tempted many to adopt this rather benevolent view of their own role in the world. So when faced with the failure of inspections in the early 1990s, they decided to take care of it themselves. That was, in my view, where the doctrine of counter-proliferation took hold, of which the prime example previously had been the Israeli attack on the Iraqi reactor in 1981.

Proponents of this view argued that whatever the cost, whatever the means, it was their obligation to prevent proliferation. And many of them shared not just disdain but contempt for international law, contempt for treaties, contempt for international institutions.

Then came the Iraq war, and with it the disappointment that there were no weapons of mass destruction. The intelligence was wrong. International inspectors came closer to the truth than did the intelligence agencies of the major powers. A whole war and tragedy followed this resort to the military. After that was the Lebanon affair, once again demonstrating the limitations of military action.

One would think this approach would be discredited, but there remain adherents who approach the Iran confrontation with the same core beliefs. Some have even sought to enlist international inspectors by, for example, repeating IAEA statements that it cannot guarantee or testify that there are no hidden nuclear installations in Iran.

Well, can the IAEA guarantee there are no hidden nuclear installations in Algeria, or in South Korea, or anywhere else? I learned, together with Mohammed ElBaradei, that if we carry out very extensive inspections, then chances are that if we do not find anything it is because there is nothing. But there is never a 100 percent guarantee. The people who were negative to Security Council–mandated inspections in Iraq in 2002 and 2003 and ignored their results are the same people who today seem opposed to diplomacy and dialogue (without preconditions) to seek assurance that Iran's activities remain peaceful.

The Iraq war and other events have shown that this approach cannot be sustained. The Romans did not permanently succeed, and the Americans cannot either. The great lesson of the Iraq war, and also of the Lebanon experience, is that this approach does not work. To paraphrase Robert Kagan, it is not Mars but Venus that will succeed, it is the European Union model that will work. Kofi Annan used to say that diplomacy may need to be backed up by strength. And that is true. But we have had over the last period a tremendous over-reliance on the military and we need to get back to an organized system. We still keep our weapons in different European countries, but we are getting away from any use of weapons against each other.

Why, after decades of détente and the end of the Cold War, is there a need for such enormous military preparations? Taiwan's status is a substantial issue with dangerous potential for armed conflict, but apart from that I do not really see any big threats. There are civil wars, wars in the Middle East and in Africa, but those are containable. Apart from these, where are the big sources of conflict today?

As human beings we have not become any wiser or kinder over the years, but there is a big change: we have come much closer to one another. We cannot fight SARS, or avian flu, or global warming, or any number of problems except through international cooperation, and that holds true whether you like or dislike a given country. Those who do not want to accept international organization and a global system of norms will have to be dragged into the twenty-first century screaming and kicking, to paraphrase Adlai Stevenson. The expansion of the rule of law is inevitable, I believe, and as applicable to the question of armaments as to any other.

8.

MARKET-FORTIFIED NONPROLIFERATION

Henry D. Sokolski

A PECULIAR CONSENSUS

One of the oddities of the current nuclear crisis posed by North Korea and Iran's civilian nuclear energy programs is how little these countries' diplomats disagree with ours about their right to almost any nuclear activity, even if it brings them to the very brink of acquiring nuclear weapons. The depth of this agreement might be surprising, given that it is widely understood that there is no way to detect military diversions from key nuclear activities (such as making nuclear fuel) early enough to prevent a state from breaking out and building a bomb. Nor does it seem to matter that developing nuclear power programs makes little or no economic sense for many countries seeking to do so.

According to the prevailing view in Washington, Pyongyang, Tehran, and beyond, all states have a per se right to any and all nuclear activities and materials, no matter how unnecessary or dangerous—so long as they are declared to and occasionally visited by international inspectors. This principle is enshrined, these diplomats insist, in Article IV of the Nuclear Non-Proliferation Treaty (NPT), which recognizes that all non-nuclear weapons states have an "inalienable right" to develop, produce, and research the "peaceful applications of nuclear energy."

As such, North Korea's sin was not that it built a plant that could process many bombs' worth of nuclear fuel, or that it operated a reactor disconnected from its electrical grid and optimized it to produce weapons-usable plutonium. All of this was permissible.

What was impermissible was North Korea's decision to block in-spectors from having full access to these facilities. Similarly, Iran's crime was not that it began enriching uranium (a process that can be used to make either reactor fuel or bombs) even before it had a single large reactor on line, or that it imported nuclear weapons de-sign information. Instead, it was Iran's failure to declare all its nucle-ar activities in a timely manner to the International Atomic Energy Agency (IAEA).

The inanity of this rather affected view of the nuclear rules was on display in a statement by President Bush's national security ad-viser, who explained that "although Iran had a right to enrich ura-nium," the United States was hoping that Iran would see that it was in its own best interest to exercise that right outside of its borders, in Russia. Not surprisingly, the Iranians, who want to develop a nucle-ar weapons option, simply disagreed.

THE UNSUSTAINABLE STATUS QUO

The consequences of continuing to interpret NPT rights and obli-gations in such a lenient fashion are clear. As UN secretary-general Kofi Annan noted at the 2005 NPT Review Conference:

> The regime will not be sustainable if scores more States develop the most sensitive phases of the fuel cycle and are equipped with the technology to produce nuclear weapons on short notice—and, of course, each individual State which does this only will leave others to feel that they must do the same. This would increase all of the risks—of nuclear ac-cident, of trafficking, of terrorist use, and of use by states themselves.[1]

It is for this reason that experts have tried to offer new ideas that might allow nuclear power to spread without increasing the prospect of further nuclear proliferation. The most fashionable of these proposals, pushed by the IAEA and the United States under its Global Nuclear Energy Partnership (GNEP), focus on assuring nations a steady supply of nuclear fuel. These assured supply pro-posals are touted as a way to keep nations from acquiring nuclear fuel–making plants of their own.[2] The question is how this is to be accomplished.

In the past decade, access to foreign nuclear fuel has been denied to many countries, including India, Iraq, North Korea, and now, Iran. These states were denied access, though, because of their nonproliferation misbehavior. As for assuring against economic disruptions by guaranteeing access to "affordable" nuclear fuel, the problem of subsidies arises; while societies may view arts or dairy cows or rail service as so socially valuable as to warrant public subsidy, the international community has a strong interest in drawing the line against subsidies in the risky energy sector. Why should any nation enjoy guaranteed access to nuclear fuel at anything but "competitive market prices"? After all, the cost of nuclear fuel is among the very least of the life cycle costs associated with the production of nuclear electricity.

If one makes nuclear fuel available at "affordable" (that is, subsidized) prices, what exactly is being secured from the fuel customer in exchange? At a minimum, there is a problem in harping on the need to guarantee fuel access as part of an effort to dissuade nations from acquiring the means to make their own fuel: it puts undue emphasis on the need for fuel, as if it was difficult to get or to stockpile in advance. In fact, nuclear fuel is easy to acquire, and suggesting otherwise unintentionally helps nations justify spending to assure their own supply even when it makes little or no economic sense to do so.[3] Again, once you concede states have a per se right to make nuclear fuel, and get to the very brink of making bombs, they are unlikely to give up that right for *any* promised guarantee or subsidy.

What else, then, can be done to reverse the trend toward "peaceful" nuclear weapons proliferation? I would like to suggest two things that have not yet been tried.

A MORE SENSIBLE READING

The first step we could make to turn things around is to get members of the NPT to read its rights and restrictions in a more sensible and stringent fashion. The NPT actually makes no mention of nuclear fuel-making, reprocessing, or enrichment. In fact, when Spain, Romania, Brazil, and Mexico all tried in the late 1960s to get NPT negotiators to include an explicit reference to "the entire fuel cycle," including fuel-making, as a per se right, each of their proposals was turned down.[4] At the time, the Swedish representative even suggested that rules needed to be established to *prevent* nations from getting into such dangerous activities since there seemed no clear way to prevent nations from either diverting the fuel or converting their fuel-making plants very quickly to make bombs.[5] The NPT was designed to share the "benefits of the application of peaceful nuclear energy" and it made no sense to have the NPT protect uneconomical propositions that were unnecessary and that could bring states to the brink of having bombs.[6]

Delegates at the time also understood that when a nuclear energy application did not offer clear economic benefits, there was no clear right to demand it under the NPT. A clear case in point was the NPT's handling of peaceful nuclear explosives, which turned out to be so dangerous and impossible to safeguard that the treaty spoke only about sharing the "potential benefits" of peaceful nuclear explosives. No effort, however, was ever made to request or to offer such nuclear explosives because they were so costly to use that no clear economic benefit could be found.[7]

Finally, in no case did the framers of the NPT believe that the inalienable right to develop, research, or produce peaceful nuclear energy should allow states to contravene the NPT restrictions designed to prevent the proliferation of nuclear weapons. These restrictions are contained in Articles I, II, and III of the treaty. Article I prohibits nuclear weapons states "assist[ing], encourag[ing], or induc[ing] any non-weapons state to manufacture or otherwise acquire" nuclear weapons. Article II prohibits non-weapons states from acquiring in any way nuclear explosives or seeking "any assistance" in their manufacture. Together, these two prohibitions suggest that the NPT bans the transfer not only of actual nuclear explosives, but also of any nuclear technology or materials that could "assist, encourage or induce" non-weapons states to "manufacture or otherwise acquire" them.[8]

If there was any doubt on this point, the NPT also requires all non-weapons states to apply safeguards against all of their nuclear facilities and holdings of special nuclear materials. The purpose of these nuclear inspections, according to the treaty, is "verification of the fulfillment of [a state's] obligations assumed under this Treaty with a view to preventing diversion of nuclear energy from peaceful uses to nuclear weapons."[9] At the time of the treaty's drafting it was hoped a way could be found to assure such safeguards. However, it was not assumed that such techniques already existed or that they would inevitably emerge.[10]

We now know that this hope was misplaced. Japan's experience with recycling plutonium from spent reactor fuel highlights the problem. On January 27, 2003, Japanese nuclear officials admitted that they had "lost" 206 kilograms of nuclear weapons usable plutonium at their Tokai-mura pilot reprocessing plant, which is under IAEA inspections. This is enough material to make over forty crude nuclear bombs. Where this plutonium went is still unknown. The plant's operators claimed that 90 kilograms "probably" was diluted into the aqueous reprocessing waste, and another 30 kilograms may have been dissolved into other waste elements during reprocessing. They offered no explanation as to where the remaining 86 kilograms of plutonium might have gone. Perhaps, they suggested, it was never even produced.

In response to these revelations, the IAEA made no demand that the Japanese shut down Tokai-mura to track the missing material by cleaning it out. Instead, the IAEA's director-general merely noted that the IAEA had no information that would suggest that any nuclear material had been "diverted from the facility." It later was revealed that the IAEA first learned of accounting shortfalls at the plant five years earlier, but had chosen to take no action. Japanese officials, meanwhile, were reluctant to admit to the losses publicly. Since then, the Japanese opened a much larger reprocessing facility at another site, which experts estimate is likely to "lose" some 240 kilograms of plutonium *every year*.[11]

Nor is the problem of knowing precisely how much weapons usable material a nuclear facility has produced limited to plutonium reprocessing or plutonium fuel fabrication plants.[12] Centrifuge uranium enrichment plants present comparable problems. Like reprocessing and plutonium fuel fabrication plants, which constantly produce or handle weapons-usable plutonium, uranium enrichment facilities can be converted to produce a bomb's worth of weapons-grade uranium so quickly (a matter of a few days) that little can be done to intervene and prevent the uranium from being hijacked for illicit use. Similarly, it is extremely difficult for inspectors to know precisely how much material a given plant might actually be able to produce, or to keep track of the many hundreds of tons of material it might make.[13] As a result, there are ways these plants can be operated to conceal illicit production of weapons-usable uranium from IAEA inspectors.[14]

Properly understood, then, it is not possible to safeguard these nuclear fuel-making activities. There is no question that IAEA inspectors can look at or monitor them. But they cannot detect the diversion of enough material to make a bomb early enough to prevent the diversion from being completed. Nor does it make sense to permit countries that might be hiding covert nuclear fuel-making plants to have large reactors. Most large reactors need lightly enriched fuel and all produce large amounts of spent fuel laden with nuclear weapons-usable plutonium. These fresh and spent fuels, in turn, can be seized and used to acquire nuclear weapons fuel with so little warning time as to defeat any effort to safeguard them.[15]

TURNING THE SHIP AROUND

What, then, is the bottom line? Any sound reading of the NPT would argue *against* the current dominant view that all states have a per se right to any and all nuclear materials and activities so long as they declare them, claim they are for peaceful purposes, and allow IAEA inspectors occasionally to visit them.

To some extent, U.S. and allied officials recognize this. A senior U.S. State Department representative to the NPT Review Conference in 2005, for example, noted that the NPT does not obligate nuclear supplier states to transfer nuclear fuel-making technologies since such aid would possibly violate Article I.[16] Moreover, the French government has argued since 2004 that nuclear fuel-making technology should be transferred only to countries that have a clear "energy need," a "credible nuclear energy program," and "an economically rational plan for developing such projects."[17] It has been Iran's inability to meet any of these criteria that has caused the French to question the sincerity of Tehran's claim to have an inalienable right to make its own nuclear fuel. This same concern with the lack of economic rationality also prompted a detailed critique from senior State Department officials.[18]

Yet, for all the support that a select number of officials in the U.S. and allied capitals now afford to a sounder reading of the NPT's "inalienable right," there are a far greater number who back the conventional view. Thus, President Bush and senior State Department officials have repeatedly contended that the NPT has a major "loophole" that supports a per se right for states to make nuclear fuel and thereby come within days of acquiring nuclear weapons.[19] The State Department's legal division, moreover, has been emphatic in supporting this view.[20]

Why, after the nuclear fuel-making activities of North Korea, Iraq, and Iran, is the current view so entrenched? The simple answer is history. The United States and its key allies have long condoned the nuclear fuel-making of so many of its key allies and friends who do not yet have nuclear weapons—countries such as Germany, the Netherlands, Japan, Brazil, Argentina, Australia, and Ukraine—that it is now very difficult to reverse course. In a very real sense, public officials have chosen to make their past mistakes hereditary.

This suggests it will take a good deal of time to convince NPT states to read the treaty's provisions in a much firmer fashion. This brings us to the second effort that should be taken in the interim in order to accelerate such a turnaround—forcing nuclear operators to own up to the full costs of nuclear power.

A PROPER ACCOUNTING

The most dangerous nuclear projects, it turns out, are also the most economically uncompetitive. These projects include nuclear power plants in oil and natural gas–rich nations (for example, Iran) or states that lack a large electrical grid (North Korea). They also include nuclear fuel-making plants in countries or regions lacking a large number of reactors (any state outside of China, Russia, Japan, the European Union, and the United States). Moreover, a nuclear facility that is built in the wrong way and in the wrong place runs much higher risks of nuclear accidents and vulnerabilities to nuclear theft and terrorist attacks.

As it is, most of the key issues related to nuclear facilities—financial, insurance, proliferation, safety, and physical security—are heavily influenced (or entirely decided) by governmental policies, regulation, and subsidies. The weight of government intervention in these issues is overwhelmingly favorable to supporting nuclear activities. Governments, by underwriting risks and providing a safety net against externalities, are, in effect, subsidizing nuclear programs. If, on the other hand, a much more accurate counting of all of nuclear power's hidden costs relating to these issues were required, it would be possible to question the purpose and value of dangerous, uneconomical nuclear undertakings much earlier, and to discourage governments from supporting them.

Fortunately, there is an attractive political vehicle for demanding such an accounting. The international movement to reduce greenhouse gas emissions continues to gain momentum, and there is broad-based agreement that these cuts should be conducted in the most cost effective manner.

In order to achieve such reductions, the European Union (EU) has already created an emissions cap and trading scheme, and discourages member governments from subsidizing their energy sector. The EU is discovering that its own emissions cap and trading scheme can be effective only if there is true transparency concerning the full costs of different energy options (that is, that the cost of any given energy option reflect the full environmental and security costs as well as the direct and indirect government subsidies). The United States and other countries are sure to back into this insight as they consider how to control their emissions.[21]

Toward this end and to assure more restrained promotion of nuclear power, four steps should be taken right away.

- *First, the world's major nations (including both signatories and observers) should live up to the open market and full costing principles they have already endorsed in the Energy Charter Treaty and the Global Energy Charter for Sustainable Development, and apply these principles to international commerce in electrical power plants.* Here, winning bids in any national competition for an electrical power system should go not to the most costly or the most subsidized project, but rather to the option that provides the best value once the full costs for producing a desired amount of clean electricity are determined. This practice should be used as a springboard to encourage nations to open up their electrical generation markets, account for all the costs (internal and external) of any given bid, and accept the lowest bidder—which more often than not will be a non-nuclear electrical generation option.[22]

- *Second, to meet tough greenhouse gas emission goals, large power-producing states must recognize that a consumption tax of some sort on greenhouse gas-generating fuels will be necessary.* Proposed legislation to impose a cost for emitting greenhouse gases is already before Congress. In several years, some form of tax is likely to be imposed in the United States and other economically advanced states.

  The specific attributes of any such tax matter. It ought to be made progressive, with rebates for citizens who are poor. It also should be kept simple by taxing the carbon content in fuels rather than trying to monitor and tax the emissions of companies and consumers who might burn the fuel. In addition, tax neutrality is desirable to keep governments from using whatever money is raised to again subsidize specific fuel types. Finally, the tax should be accompanied by legal requirements that all subsidies now in place for nuclear power, natural gas, oil, clean coal, and renewables be identified, and that all fuel-specific subsidies be eliminated as soon as possible. It seems clear that anything less would only stack the deck higher in favor of nuclear energy against safer alternatives such as natural gas, increased efficiency programs, coal with carbon sequestration, hydropower, and renewable resources that may well turn out to be much cheaper. As the British government noted in its most recent energy review, published July 11, 2006, it would be appropriate and practical for firms building and operating nuclear electricity-generating plants to assume the full costs of financing, insuring, and decommissioning these plants if a proper tax or price was placed on carbon emissions.[23]

- *Third, trade zones that have enforcement powers should penalize any large electrical power production program that is enjoying national government subsidies.* In the case of the EU, this means taking far more seriously the formal complaints that have been raised about the French government's construction of a nuclear power plant in Finland, to which the Finnish and French governments have lent financial support.[24] Thought also should be given now, before the current Kyoto regime is to be updated in 2012, to how penalizing governments for subsidizing electrical generation projects might be made a priority not only for the EU, but also for other trading zones and the World Trade Organization.

Under such a market regime, nations that choose to subsidize any particular form of energy production would be called to account for undermining international trade and economic fairness. If they subsidized nuclear activities, they also could also be collared for threatening international security. Certainly, subsidizing nuclear fuel-making makes no economic sense. Countries might claim that they need to make fuel for energy independence, but this is nonsense: the reactors and the fuel-making plants that such an effort requires would have to be imported, in most cases along with raw uranium to fuel them.

- *Fourth, states keen on promoting nonproliferation should make a sounder reading of the NPT's "inalienable right" to "peaceful" nuclear energy a priority going into the current round of 2010 NPT Review Conference preparatory meetings.* Here, in addition to the safeguards qualifications inherent to the NPT's discussion of this "right," it would make sense to emphasize the NPT's discussion of sharing the "benefits" of the application of peaceful nuclear energy and of peaceful nuclear explosives. The latter were never thought to be significant. As such, no sharing of peaceful nuclear explosive benefits ever took place. We need to consider what the benefits of the applications of peaceful nuclear energy clearly are.[25] There is no question that isotopes for agriculture and medicine have been a major economic boon. As for nuclear power, the net benefits remain disputed. For nuclear fuel-making, it is even more questionable.

We should be willing to get the answers even if it means having less international promotion of nuclear power. At a minimum, the NPT should no longer be used as a legal justification for nations to subsidize dangerous, uneconomical nuclear projects that bring them to the brink of acquiring bombs. Instead, a proper reading of the treaty and its various qualifications to exercising the right to "peaceful nuclear energy" should make any state's subsidization of large nuclear projects cause for suspicion and, if such subsidization is persistent, for alarm.

Conclusion

Would a market-fortified NPT regime of this sort end the use or expansion of nuclear power? No. As noted, a carbon tax would actually favor nuclear power if it is clearly cheaper than clean coal, natural gas, hydropower, and renewable alternatives.

Would it eliminate the problems posed by a nuclear-ready Iran or North Korea? Unfortunately, again, the answer is no. Those problems can now be dealt with only by military, economic, and diplomatic efforts to squeeze Iran and North Korea—such as those used on the Soviet Union during the Cold War.

But the market fortified system suggested would help prevent Iran and North Korea's patently uneconomic ploys from becoming an international nuclear model for countries now professing an earnest desire to back peaceful nuclear power development. These countries include Indonesia, Libya, Saudi Arabia, South Korea, Nigeria, Egypt, Turkey, Morocco, Jordan, and Yemen (each of which are bizarrely receiving active U.S. or IAEA cooperative technical assistance to complete their first large power stations[26]).

Also, unlike the situation under today's interpretation of the NPT, which ignores suspicious "civilian" nuclear undertakings even when they obviously lack any economic rationale, the market fortified system described would help flag worrisome nuclear activities far sooner—well before a nation came anywhere near making bombs. Such an approach, in short, would encourage an NPT-centered world worthy of the name, a world in which the NPT would restrain the further spread of nuclear weapons-related technology rather than foster it.

9.

REVERSING THE SPREAD OF NUCLEAR WEAPONS

Carl Robichaud

America's most acute national security threat today, as it has been for the past half-century, is a catastrophic attack with nuclear weapons. Yet the current U.S. approach to preventing the spread of nuclear weapons lacks strategic coherence. This failure is minimally a result of insufficient prioritization or poor execution, though these problems exist as well; fundamentally, it results from a strategic miscalculation.

Washington's attempt to cling to an unsustainable nuclear status-quo is counterproductive and puts American lives and interests at risk. The end of the Cold War presented the nuclear powers with an opportunity to rethink the role of nuclear weapons in their security strategies. France, Britain, and China all deemphasized nuclear weapons, each arriving at a different formulation for minimum deterrence. The same movement had momentum in the United States and Russia as well, as Presidents Yeltsin, Bush, and Clinton built on the Reykjavik summit reached by Gorbachev and Reagan to negotiate substantial cuts in nuclear arsenals and eliminate entire classes of weapons. The belief was gaining ground among political and military leaders that while we may have lived with these weapons as a necessary evil during the Cold War, doing so was no longer necessary or desirable.

Today we are further from this understanding than ever. Russia recently announced it might withdraw from the 1987 Intermediate-Range Nuclear Forces Treaty, France declared that it might respond to terrorist attacks with nuclear weapons, and Britain voted to extend its use of Trident submarines into the foreseeable future. Washington, for its part, has not only failed to lead the way toward a nuclear-free world but also has actively impeded the efforts of others to do so. America's current national security strategy emphasizes freedom of action, asserts the utility of nuclear weapons, and advocates new offensive and defensive weapons systems.

The irony of this approach is that in terms of pure realpolitik, no nation would benefit more from a policy that deemphasizes nuclear weapons and establishes a framework to verifiably eliminate them. The United States is at once the least reliant upon nuclear deterrence (because of its overwhelming conventional deterrent) and most susceptible to its sway (since a "rogue" state with a few deliverable nuclear weapons could deter all America's military might). As a recent and much-cited *Wall Street Journal* op-ed by George Shultz, William Perry, Henry Kissinger, and Sam Nunn argued, America would be stronger and safer in a world free of nuclear weapons, and a wise approach would be to recast its national security strategy to reflect this goal.[1]

THE DUAL THREATS

Today the most immediate security threats facing the United States are interrelated: nuclear terrorism and nuclear proliferation. These two threats create a perilous dynamic that cannot be resolved by the United States and its allies acting alone—the means to produce these weapons are simply too diffuse. The best defense is the web of nonproliferation mechanisms that have served remarkably well over the past half-century. But—as the unmasking of Iraq's clandestine program in 1991 demonstrated—these are no longer sufficient. Strengthening them will require support not only from likeminded states but also from those that are highly skeptical of America's motives.

Nuclear Non-Proliferation Treaty (NPT) inspection mechanisms, for example, must be fortified to permit more intrusive and comprehensive inspections so that civilian nuclear technology cannot be diverted. Its existing loopholes will not be closed, however, until the parties to the treaty willingly accept further restrictions on their rights under the treaty. Since all but five of these signatories are non-nuclear weapons states—many of which are cynical about the motives of the nuclear weapons states—progress on this issue will advance only if the nuclear weapons states can convincingly demonstrate that they are upholding their end of the deal.

The NPT was negotiated in 1968 as a bargain: non-nuclear states agreed to forgo nuclear weapons in return for access to peaceful nuclear technologies and a promise that nuclear weapons states would "pursue negotiations in good faith on effective measures relating to cessation of the nuclear arms race at an early date and to nuclear disarmament."[2]

The current impasse, in which nuclear weapons states focus exclusively on proliferation while non-nuclear weapons states focus on disarmament, often seems irresolvable, but it is not. An opportunity exists for nuclear weapons states to leverage deep and verifiable cuts in their arsenals into more stringent controls on nuclear materials and technologies. Seizing this opportunity will require a new U.S. willingness to accept limitations on its prerogatives in order to gain longer-term benefits.

THREE INSEPARABLE PROBLEMS

The challenge facing America can be boiled down to three distinct, but ultimately inseparable, problems:

1. *the vast stocks of nuclear material,* especially in the former Soviet Union, that remain vulnerable to theft and diversion;
2. *loopholes in the international nonproliferation regime* that, unless mended, could lead to a world replete with nuclear-armed states; and
3. *the hard cases,* Iran and North Korea, which appear determined to acquire nuclear weapons even in the face of high costs.

In response to this multifaceted challenge, the current administration has focused almost exclusively on the third problem, which it has defined as "rogue" regimes defying an international consensus against proliferation. This approach shines the spotlight on the activities of Iran and North Korea, with little attention to the broader problems posed by arsenals in India, Pakistan, or Israel; the tens of thousands of weapons in Russia, the United States, France, Britain, and China; or the potential for dozens of states to "go nuclear" should the political winds shift.

The current approach manifests itself in narrow and tactical measures rather than a coherent strategy to repair structural problems within the nonproliferation regime. For example, the Proliferation

Security Initiative (PSI) usefully facilitates efforts among sixty countries to share intelligence, coordinate export controls, and interdict illegal shipments, but to be sustainable must be better-integrated into international law and existing institutions. The administration's nuclear deal with India may provide bilateral strategic benefits, but does so at the cost of facilitating a larger Indian arsenal and encouraging Russia and China to offer similar packages to others. U.S. missile defenses could provide a hedge against nuclear attack, but will spur other countries to develop countermeasures by enhancing or enlarging their arsenals. The invasion of Iraq ensured that Saddam Hussein would never acquire nuclear weapons, but has proved deeply counterproductive and prohibitively expensive.

These narrow fixes might be considered successful if the nuclear status quo was sustainable. Unfortunately, advocates of piecemeal solutions ignore the fact that there is not a single nuclear crisis, or even several crises—there is instead an unstable system that seems ordained to spin off crisis after crisis, indefinitely. Iraq and North Korea are two manifestations of the nuclear problem, but they will not be the last. Terrorist networks and criminal syndicates, which have tried with increasing frequency and sophistication to attain nuclear arms, are another product of this status quo. The responses to these crises, which involve the world's most dangerous weapons, demand zero tolerance for error.

The notion of a stable status quo is a myth. As the independent Canberra Commission stated in 1995, the situation in which "nuclear weapons are held by a handful of states which insist that these weapons provide unique security benefits, and yet reserve uniquely to themselves the right to own them" is "highly discriminatory and thus unstable; it cannot be sustained." This vulnerability is accentuated by loopholes in the NPT, which some states interpret as permitting them to come a screwdriver's turn from the Bomb. Historically, each state that has acquired nuclear weapons has done so to counter another nuclear power or to gain an elite status symbol, a pattern that leads the Canberra Commission to warn that "the possession of nuclear weapons by any state is a constant stimulus to other states to acquire them."[3]

Without a change in the current dynamics, we seem headed toward a nuclear attack by terrorists on American soil and toward a world of twenty or thirty nuclear states. These futures may be preventable, but only by decisive movement in a new direction.

A Comprehensive Approach

The United States needs a comprehensive strategy to address the three tiers of threats:

1. *secure dangerous materials:* a better-coordinated, broader, and fully funded effort to secure loose nuclear weapons and materials internationally;
2. *reinforce nonproliferation mechanisms:* a new bargain to repair the NPT; and
3. *engage realistically with the hard cases:* an expansion beyond the current focus and toward a comprehensive resolution of the confrontations with North Korea and Iran.

Each of these steps requires strenuous engagement by Washington with both its allies and adversaries.

Secure Dangerous Materials

The theft and trafficking of nuclear materials is not a hypothetical threat but a documented reality. The Nuclear Threat Initiative maintains a list of "anecdotes of insecurity," which offers sobering details from dozens of confirmed incidents and hints at the breadth of possible threats.[4]

After September 11, the president observed that America's greatest threat "lies at the perilous crossroads of radicalism and technology," but the administration's attention has focused almost exclusively on confronting radical groups and the states that harbor them, thereby neglecting the supply side of the intersection.

Right now, the supply side offers the greatest returns. Fifteen years of cooperative programs have reduced but not eliminated the threat from weapons materials in Russia and the former Soviet republics, where a vast nuclear infrastructure once spanned ten "closed" nuclear cities and employed a million people. In securing these materials, a 99 percent success rate could still mean catastrophic failure; with security upgrades on only half of Russia's nuclear buildings housing weapons-usable nuclear materials, we are nowhere near that level of confidence.[5] We must move faster: at the current rate, the United States may not secure these weapons and materials as late as 2020.[6]

Threat reduction programs conducted by the United States and Russia, despite their remarkable track record, have not always had the full support of either government. Impediments have ranged from inadequate funding to poor interagency coordination. Most recently, liability was the issue: as initially negotiated, the program held Russia liable for any accidents that might occur, even if they were caused by American contractors. Disagreement over this clause was permitted to fester, with the entire framework salvaged only by a last minute compromise in June 2006.

The following steps would help accelerate progress in securing dangerous materials:

- *Provide leadership.* The president should appoint a senior coordinator for threat reduction, most likely seated at the National Security Council, who can resolve interagency differences and provide executive attention to the issue when needed.[7] "Today, if the president asked, at a cabinet meeting, who is responsible for preventing nuclear terrorism, six or eight hands in the room might go up, or none," Graham Allison observes.[8] Threat reduction programs depend on coordination among the Departments of Defense, Energy, and State, each of which manages overlapping components of the program. These agencies must act synchronously—dismantling a nuclear weapons research site does little to increase our security unless jobs can be found for its scientists—and simultaneously coordinate with Congress, which has complicated matters with certification requirements. And these same agencies must engage in negotiations with their Russian counterparts, some of whom suspect that threat reduction programs are a cover for espionage. Appointing a single, high-level coordinator with the confidence of the president would not solve these issues, but would make their resolution much more likely.
- *Sustain funding.* The administration should request, and Congress should deliver, an infusion of funding for threat reduction programs. Compared to other defense and homeland security spending, this modest expenditure constitutes a bargain—and perhaps the most efficient security investment in a half-trillion-dollar Pentagon budget.

  These programs cost about $1 billion in total in 2006 and have averaged $600 million per year since 1992.[9] Yet the Bush

administration's support for them has been inconsistent, and today's modest increases from pre–September 11 funding—a total of 19 percent over five years—have only occurred because
of congressional action (the president requested a 5 percent
increase during that period).[10] Even if funding were increased
from $1.1 billion to $3 billion per year—which is what the
Baker-Cutler commission and other assessments say is needed—
the investment would be a bargain compared to our other nuclear-related programs, such as the $17 billion requested this
year to maintain America's oversized nuclear arsenals or the
$11.1 billion for ballistic missile defense.[11]

Skeptics rightly argue that Russia has been a less-than-per-
fect partner in threat reduction implementation, but this does
not change the fundamental reality: these weapons will not be
secured without Moscow's consent and participation. Congress
has a fiduciary responsibility here, but certainty over every dollar spent will be little consolation if a Russian weapon finds its
way to an American city.

- *Globalize threat reduction.* Pakistan has engaged in multiple
transfers of nuclear technologies and materials, and its intelligence services have ties to radical jihadists. Less understood
is where Pakistan stores its weapons or fissile materials (which
are dispersed to reduce vulnerability to an attack by India) and
what levels of security they receive.[12] Building a fully multilateral program would allow each at-risk nation (among them
Pakistan, India, China, and Israel) to design its own nuclear security system with support—in the form of technical expertise,
funding, and standards—from an international agency backed
by broad international consensus.

- *Strengthen and internationalize nuclear attribution processes.*
While forensic technologies exist for tracing nuclear explosions
back to their source of manufacture, these capabilities are not
yet sufficiently credible. This capacity is of critical importance:
it would allow the United States and the international community to hold actors accountable should they, through malice or
neglect, pass on nuclear materials to terrorist groups or "rogue"
regimes.

The United States would improve its ability to contain and
deter nuclear terrorism if it improved its nuclear attribution capabilities. These capacities must also be better publicized if they

are to have a deterrent effect. Moreover, internationalizing the process of post-explosion assessment would increase the credibility of this process among skeptical states, and would extend the benefits of accountability to other nations.

Reinforce Nonproliferation Mechanisms

Iran, North Korea, India, Pakistan, Israel, Libya: each tear in the fabric of the nonproliferation regime reveals the tensions under which the system strains.

Today forty states possess the dual-use materials and technologies necessary to build nuclear weapons, should they decide to do so. Tomorrow this list may grow—recent expressions of interest in nuclear energy by Egypt, Saudi Arabia, Turkey, Jordan, and several Persian Gulf states, presumably inspired by Iran's progress toward a fuel cycle, suggest that latent nuclear capabilities could soon spread. Moreover, international networks that trade in illicit goods, of which the A. Q. Khan network is only the most notorious, make it increasingly possible for states or groups without advanced nuclear programs to procure weapons technology.

Far more stringent nuclear controls are needed, but, as noted earlier, these cannot and will not be achieved in the current climate. The 2005 NPT Review Conference starkly demonstrated that seeking concessions from non-nuclear weapons states is a non-starter unless nuclear weapons states show seriousness about their NPT disarmament commitments.

A more sustainable nuclear regime cannot be achieved without the United States in the vanguard. Yet Washington's actions over the past decade have deeply undermined its credibility. The Bush administration's December 2001 Nuclear Posture Review called for a "a range of options" not merely to deter but also "to defeat any aggressor" using nuclear weapons, while the National Nuclear Security Administration (the Energy Department agency in charge of stockpile stewardship) launched a Readiness Campaign "to revitalize the nuclear weapons manufacturing infrastructure."[13]

Meanwhile, Washington repudiated the thirteen-step roadmap that the 2000 NPT Review Conference had unanimously endorsed for implementing the Article VI disarmament clause.[14] These policy reversals suggested to other states that the United States has no intention of ever eliminating its weapons, that it sees nuclear weapons as legitimate to use in conflicts (unlike chemical and biological weapons), and that it in fact intends to strengthen and expand its nuclear capabilities.

The Bush administration asserts that it has made deep cuts in the U.S. arsenal, citing its 2002 agreement with Moscow to reduce its nuclear arsenal by 2012.[15] However, the Washington-Moscow pact is a sharp departure from the Strategic Arms Reduction Treaties (START) that it replaces. It contains none of the verification measures that are the backbone of arms control treaties, excludes tactical nuclear weapons, and requires no destruction of warheads, but only their removal from delivery systems. Moreover, it expires the day it comes into effect, legally permitting each nation to redeploy its stockpile immediately. In short, the pact shifts the bilateral nuclear framework onto a new track where verification does not exist and the destruction of warheads is optional—in other words, a track to nowhere.

Meanwhile, the current administration has increased America's reliance upon nuclear arms to achieve political and security objectives. The purported rationale for keeping these weapons is that, while they are difficult to use effectively, their mere presence in the arsenal provides a useful "strategic ambiguity" that could serve to deter terrorists from using chemical weapons or states from pursuing non-nuclear aggression. In reality, however, it strains the imagination to conjure up a scenario in which American interests would be served by the use of a nuclear weapon. The Kosovo and Iraq air wars demonstrated that America's conventional airpower is sufficient to achieve every deterrent aim for which a nuclear weapon would be considered.

The remaining role ascribed to nuclear weapons is their utility in destroying deeply fortified underground bunkers. Yet the notion that a nuclear "bunker buster" could be used surgically is a myth. "Current experience and empirical predictions indicate that earth-penetrator weapons cannot penetrate to depths required for total containment of the effects of a nuclear explosion," a National Academy of Sciences study noted, calculating that civilian casualties from an attack in or near urban areas "can range from thousands to more than a million."[16] Other critics note that a bunker buster would still require high, and possibly unrealistic, precision in target selection, have a low likelihood of success, and result in devastating fallout.[17]

Even such a tactical use of nuclear weapons would shatter the sixty-year nuclear taboo, blackening America's image in the world and inviting future asymmetrical retaliation. When examined closely, nuclear weapons have no utility in today's world other than the deterrence of other nuclear arms.

On the other hand, a world free of nuclear weapons would benefit all nations, but especially the United States, which is among the most likely targets for nuclear terrorists. Washington should reverse its march toward a more aggressive nuclear posture and adopt a nuclear stance more in line with its international obligations, its nonproliferation objectives, and common sense. The United States should take the following steps:

- *Deemphasize nuclear weapons in security planning.* Starting with a bottom-up nuclear posture review, the next administration should critically reassess whether nuclear weapons remain central to its security strategy. If they are not, it should adopt the position that their only legitimate purpose is to deter other nuclear weapons.

    Washington will need to take several long-overdue steps to convince others that it is serious: affirming that it will never use nuclear weapons first; affirming that it will never use them against non-nuclear states; restarting the process for ratification of the Comprehensive Test Ban Treaty (CTBT); prohibiting the development of new nuclear weapons; and reducing the alert status of its arsenals. The CTBT is of particular symbolic and substantive significance since it suggests the long-term direction of American nuclear policy. Today the treaty appears dead in the water, but recent technical advances and a renewed sense of urgency make this an issue ripe for a renewed bipartisan push.

    The United States should also engage in negotiations for a new nuclear weapons treaty to succeed the Moscow pact—negotiations that would culminate in a treaty to control tactical nuclear weapons and verifiably reduce both countries' strategic arsenals to around 500 deployed warheads. Defense analyst Lawrence Korb calculates that "shifting to a deployed arsenal of 600 warheads with another 400 in reserve—an arsenal fully capable of deterring known threats and hedging against unforeseen contingencies—would generate $13 billion in savings" every year.[18]

- *Reaffirm America's commitment to Article VI.* The United States has backed away from its commitment to nuclear disarmament, arguing that because the clause citing nuclear disarmament places it in the context of general disarmament, nuclear weapons states are under no legal obligation to eliminate their arsenals (though it argues that its recent reductions are nevertheless consistent with the spirit of Article VI).[19] This novel interpretation is divisive and counterproductive. A statement affirming the goal of disarmament would take international pressure off the United States and put the spotlight on other nuclear weapons states, which have tended to stand back and let the United States take the heat.

  Nuclear arms can never be "uninvented," but there are many sound proposals on how to place the world's arsenals verifiably into a state of latency. To show that it is serious about this initiative the United States should propose and fund a high-level expert commission on a nuclear-free world. The commission, structured along the lines of the 9/11 Commission or the Iraq Study Group, would bring bipartisan and international experts together to examine potential paths to disarmament.

- *Tighten nuclear controls.* The U.S. negotiating team arrived at the 2005 NPT Review Conference with a blueprint for tightening nuclear controls, including universalizing adherence to the Additional Protocol and making it a condition of nuclear supply, closing an NPT loophole by restricting enrichment and processing technology, and creating a safeguards committee on the IAEA Board of Governors.[20] These plans were dead before they were announced, however, because of the rift between nuclear and non-nuclear weapons states over their respective NPT commitments. A recommitment by the United States to its Article VI obligations could create new opportunities for stringent measures against proliferation.

- *Seek stronger controls over the nuclear fuel cycle.* The NPT permits signatories access to peaceful nuclear technology, a right that some states claim extends to all aspects of the nuclear fuel cycle, including uranium enrichment and spent fuel reprocessing. But nothing in the NPT provides these rights; in fact, access to any and all aspects of nuclear technology, including high-risk activities, goes against the NPT's intent.

In an ideal world, the NPT would be clarified to spell out, in no uncertain terms, that there was no inherent right to uranium enrichment. But this measure will require the sort of concerted diplomatic push that the United States could credibly conduct only with its house in order.

In the meantime, the United States should do everything it can to make it undesirable for states to acquire a full nuclear fuel cycle. One proposal that holds promise is an internationally monitored fuel bank that would ensure the secure provision and removal of nuclear fuel, at below the national cost of production, to states that forswear enrichment and reprocessing and submit to stringent safeguards.[21] This proposal would not solve the problem on its own, but it would help separate the wolves from the sheep by revealing which states were involved in uneconomical activities that make sense only in the context of developing a weapons option. Correctly implemented,[22] this program could close the loophole that Iran and others have sought to exploit and would, according to Mohammad ElBaradei, head of the IAEA, solve "at least 80 percent of the problem."[23]

The 2005 NPT Review Conference demonstrated that nonnuclear states will be reluctant to accept any of these additional restraints without assurances that the nuclear states are acting in good faith on their disarmament commitments. The United States—in defiance of its own core interests—has been the most provocative in disavowing those commitments. It will require a bold recommitment to turn the ship around.

Engage Realistically with the Hard Cases

Iran and North Korea pose two imminent threats to the nonproliferation regime. If Iran were to acquire nuclear weapons, it would discredit the nonproliferation regime and create incentives for Saudi Arabia, Egypt, and other states to advance programs of their own. The international community missed its opportunity to prevent North Korea from acquiring nuclear weapons, but its challenge today is equally critical: preventing Pyongyang from producing more weapons and dissuading it from exporting them. A full analysis of the challenges posed by these two states is beyond the scope of this brief, but they merit passing mention.

The fundamental problem with North Korea, which has perhaps a handful of nuclear weapons, has been that, thus far, nothing Washington is willing to offer is sufficient, while none of its threats are credible. These dynamics suggest that, taken in isolation, the nuclear issue may be beyond resolution. Even hawks quietly have taken the military option off the table, and sanctions can go only so far, especially when China, the linchpin to this strategy, has $2 billion of annual trade and investment in North Korea and will do nothing that could push Pyongyang over the brink. As for regime change, none of the likely outcomes are desirable: repugnant as the current government may be, the likely alternative is chaos, a failed state possessing nuclear weapons and awash in conventional arms.

So while the recent disarmament talks show some promise, a solution will be sustainable only if it goes beyond quid pro quo on nuclear issues and offers Pyongyang genuine incentives for genuine change. The North's oversized military and moribund economy are major factors in Pyongyang's behavior, and a comprehensive package of deep conventional arms cuts on the peninsula linked to economic assistance could transform the dynamics of the U.S.-North Korean relationship.[24] A deal that verifiably disarms North Korea and integrates it into the region could hardly be termed appeasement. Libya's decision to abandon its weapons programs demonstrates that serious negotiations, backed by the appropriate carrots and sticks, can yield results even with unsavory regimes.

Iran provides a different challenge. It has violated its IAEA safeguards agreement by engaging in a clandestine pilot program to enrich uranium and has developed, through legal and illicit activities, capacities that could lead to nuclear weapons. Its apparent readiness to move to weaponization is a major challenge to the nonproliferation regime.

Tehran, however, is at least several years from developing a working nuclear weapon, offering a window for diplomacy.[25] As in the case of North Korea, it is hard to imagine a solution emerging from a narrow focus on the nuclear question, the tack that the United States has tried to take in recent third-party negotiations. Instead, the United States should engage in multilateral but direct talks aimed at a comprehensive resolution that addresses a fuel-cycle agreement, economic and political relations, unfreezing of Iranian assets, security assurances, and ending Iran's support for terrorism.[26] There is no guarantee that such talks would succeed, but they have not yet been tried.

CONCLUSION

Washington's current policy approach of half-steps and tactical adjustments has not reduced the nuclear danger. Neither have costly investments in missile defenses, which provide an uncertain answer to missiles from "rogue" states and no answer whatsoever to nuclear terrorism. Unless the United States makes profound changes in its nonproliferation strategy, it could soon face a terrorist group with nuclear arms or a world of a dozen or more nuclear states.

The United States should change tack and focus on trading deep and verifiable cuts in existing arsenals for more stringent controls on nuclear materials and technologies. It should restructure its efforts to accelerate and globalize the threat reduction programs that serve as our only reliable line of defense against nuclear terrorism.

The change begins with the recognition that loose nuclear materials, in the words of the Baker-Cutler report five years ago, still pose "the most urgent unmet national security threat to the United States."[27] It also requires recognizing that nuclear weapons have no role in today's world, except perhaps to deter other nuclear weapons. This reality is understood by the dozens of generals, admirals, and political leaders who have recognized that nuclear weapons are morally abhorrent and politically useless.[28] They are justified as a hedge against some unspecified threat, but their existence perpetuates and exacerbates the risks they are purported to counter. The only long-term solution to the nuclear dilemma is the elimination of all nuclear weapons, a position that resounds with the vast majority of the public[29] and could anchor a progressive foreign policy vision.

APPENDIX 1

EUROPEAN PERSPECTIVE
A VIEW FROM ROME

Opening Remarks by Filippo Formica

I wish to thank The Century Foundation for sponsoring this conference and the Center for American Progress for its collaboration. I am particularly indebted to Jeff Laurenti and Joe Cirincione, without their efforts and dedication this event would not have been possible. It's a timely initiative, as we are about to start a new review cycle of the Nuclear Non-Proliferation Treaty (NPT) and this time we are not allowed to fail. This conference also demonstrates the quality of the cooperation between The Century Foundation and Italy. I also wish to thank all the distinguished participants.

Disarmament and nonproliferation are a political priority for the Italian government. This is why the Italian Ministry of Foreign Affairs decided to contribute to this event, on the occasion of Italy's return to the Security Council as a nonpermanent member. In this spirit, Foreign Minister D'Alema has requested that I convey to all of you his warmest regards.

Disarmament and nonproliferation are more than ever matters of serious concern to public opinion. On both sides of the Atlantic there is a growing consensus on the danger created by the proliferation of weapons of mass destruction (WMDs).

In the last few years the international situation has unfortunately not been marked by much success in the field of disarmament and nonproliferation. The NPT Review Conference in New York (May 2005) ended without any recommendations. Nor was the September 2005 United Nations Summit able to hold out any tangible prospects. Yet, despite these disappointments, the principles that underpin the general nonproliferation regime have never actually been challenged, and no one doubts the validity of the NPT. This indicates that the NPT continues to be considered the cornerstone of the international disarmament and nonproliferation regime.

In addition, many positive elements emerged. First, the role played by the European Union at the NPT Review Conference and the balanced and comprehensive nature of the European Common Position. Another positive element I would like to emphasize is the scope of the debate in New York in May 2005, in which many important issues were introduced. These include the need for new rules governing the nuclear fuel cycle and access to these capabilities, a more restrictive interpretation of the right of withdrawal from the NPT, and international cooperation for the elimination of weapons of mass destruction and related materials.

But the debates in New York were marked by the sharply divergent positions of countries that give absolute priority to nonproliferation and others that make nuclear disarmament a precondition.

The basis of the international nonproliferation regime is at risk of being undermined: not only are two major crises far from being solved, but also increasing tensions are jeopardizing the stability of the regime. I refer in particular to the perception that obligations under the treaties, or at least their implementation, are not balanced (nonproliferation versus disarmament, versus peaceful uses).

We must break this vicious circle and take concrete initiatives. We need a forward-looking approach, a new commitment of the international community, and a fresh start. It is important to show the political will to make concrete progress. It is time to take action and bridge the gaps.

I intend to focus on a few points.

First of all, Italy is engaged in enhancing the role of the European Union and making it more incisive and dynamic. With the adoption in December 2003 of its Non-Proliferation Strategy, under the Italian presidency, the EU became a major player in this regard. The EU strategy stresses that cooperation with the United States and other key partners is necessary to ensure a successful outcome of the global fight against proliferation. I look forward to the strengthening of this cooperation.

Which brings me to my second point: the International Atomic Energy Agency (IAEA) Additional Protocols. Without Additional Protocols in force, the effectiveness of the IAEA is seriously constrained.

The universalisation of the Additional Protocol will guarantee more effective verifications and inspections. Together with the comprehensive safeguards, the Additional Protocol must be held as the standard for IAEA verifications. In addition, the Additional Protocol should become a condition for the supply of nuclear materials and technologies; we have not yet reached an agreement on this measure. This issue must be taken up in the relevant multilateral fora.

We need to take a further step and examine the possibility of rendering the conclusion of an Additional Protocol mandatory.

Thirdly, negotiations on a Fissile Material Cutoff Treaty (FMCT) are yet another concrete action to which I would like to draw your attention. It is significant that for over ten years there has been a substantial agreement in the main multilateral fora—I am thinking above all of the Geneva Conference on Disarmament and the United Nations General Assembly—on the value-added that the FMCT would give to the nuclear nonproliferation cause.

The structured debate on FMCT held in the Conference on Disarmament last year proved extremely constructive and was marked by very interesting developments.

The drafts prepared by the United States on the FMCT and on the mandate of the Conference on Disarmament to negotiate it, while not entirely consistent with our approach to this issue—as Washington remains opposed to any reference to verification—constitute a significant contribution to the discussion.

Italy is actively promoting the debate in Geneva, the Italian permanent representative to the Conference on Disarmament has been appointed as coordinator for the FMCT.

We believe that the time has come to upgrade the level of the international commitment towards the FMCT.

Not to mention, finally, the entry into force of the Comprehensive Test Ban Treaty (CTBT); this objective must remain high on our agenda. Eight years after the nuclear tests of 1998, the North Korean nuclear test provoked sharp criticism from the international community. While it was a major setback for the cause of nonproliferation and disarmament, this event only added a sense of urgency to the entry into force of the Treaty. The entry into force of the CTBT would be an important contribution to international peace and security.

I hope that our debate will allow us to identify a road map and stimulate concrete answers to the problems that are still in front of us.

Appendix 2

Point/Counterpoint
A Nuclear Weapons–Free Iran

Speakers and their affiliations (in order of appearance):

- Richard C. Leone, The Century Foundation
- Carla Robbins, *The New York Times*
- Javad Zarif, Permanent Mission of Iran to the United Nations
- Richard Haass, the Council on Foreign Relations
- Jeffrey Laurenti, The Century Foundation
- William Potter, Center for Nonproliferation Studies
- Paolo Cotta-Ramusino, Pugwash Conferences on Science and World Affairs

LEONE: I am grateful for all the work by Joe Cirincione, who has been such a good colleague with the Center for American Progress, for making this possible. And of course my thanks especially to the Italian Foreign Ministry for their idea and support of this conference. We have heard throughout the day varying degrees of optimism and pessimism, and we've heard a lot of general conversation about arms control. In the American newspapers today, the focus is on arms control in a couple of countries and nuclear proliferation in a couple of places, and we're fortunate this afternoon to have with us people who can discuss that with great authority.

Our panel is very distinguished. It includes Richard Haass, the President of the Council on Foreign Relations, who served both Presidents Bush and is a scholar of foreign policy in his own right. And Ambassador Javad Zarif, the Permanent Representative to the United Nations from Iran. They will be candid, but this is an on-the-record session, and I want to make sure everybody understands that we're not operating on Council rules.

To moderate this discussion, we have Carla Robbins, the deputy Editorial Page editor of the *New York Times,* and so without further ado, Carla.

ROBBINS: Thank you very much. I think we've decided rather than having opening remarks, I'm just going to ask you a few softball questions to start. (laughter) And then everybody else can lob their softballs as well. I want to start with the ambassador. We can all discuss—and I'm sure we will—what the perceptions are of Iran's intention with its pursuit of a nuclear fuel production capability. But I suppose my most basic question is that Iran has been ordered by the Security Council to suspend enrichment. And more than six months have passed and you're still doing it. So the question is why, and how can you justify what basically is a total rejection of international law?

ZARIF: Well, first of all let me say that if this is a softball, what will be the hardball? (laughter)

ROBBINS: You can imagine what my question would have been like if I were at the [Wall Street] *Journal.*

ZARIF: And I expected no less from you. But I want to first of all thank the organizers for having organized this wonderful event, and I'm sure it helps to discuss these issues, even the softball issues that you raise.

The problem with the resolutions that were adopted by the Security Council has been that the resolutions were not adopted in an effort to find a resolution to the problem, but in an effort to impose pressure on Iran. If I remember it correctly, it was Ambassador Bolton who said in 2005, at AIPAC, that rest assured, that the Security Council is not the only tool in our toolbox. So if the Security Council is perceived as a tool in the toolbox, you don't expect others to treat it any differently.

Now, we need to find a resolution to this problem. Iran exercised a voluntary suspension of its enrichment activities for over two years. But unfortunately during those two years, no attempt was made in order to negotiate a solution. There were attempts to continue the negotiations, and I led the Iranian delegation in the negotiations and

I can tell you, as my personal observation, that there were attempts to continue and prolong the negotiations but there were no attempts to find a solution. We presented offers, proposals, after-proposals in order to find the solution, but unfortunately there were no takers.

So we knew that the Security Council was being mentioned from the first day as an instrument of pressure in order to bring Iran into—*compel* Iran into—accepting a demand that we thought was unreasonable and would not resolve the problem. And that is why nobody expected Iran to observe that demand, and that is what happened afterwards.

ROBBINS: So you get to pick and choose on Security Council resolutions because we have an impolitic ambassador to the UN?

ZARIF: No, we don't get to pick and choose on Security Council resolutions. In fact the United States has started that practice a long time ago, and it didn't start with Ambassador Bolton, it started a long time ago. There are many Security Council resolutions that have been left unimplemented, and there has been very little effort in order to implement them. And those are Security Council resolutions that escape U.S. veto. Now, if I tell you the number of Security Council resolutions that's already received a gesture of a U.S. veto, the numbers would have been even larger.

The problem is when we see a U.S. ambassador and the U.S. government trying to use the Security Council as an instrument of pressure. When we see a letter by the political director of the United Kingdom, who used to be my negotiating partner when I negotiated, saying that we need to use the Security Council in order to deprive Iran from its legal argument that suspension was voluntary. You see all of these and you put them together and you see that the Security Council is not a part of the solution but a part of the problem. It has been from the very first day.

The problem is if you try to continue to put blame on one country or another for not accepting the pressure that is being imposed, you will not resolve the problem. There are ways of resolving this problem and we need to look at those ways instead of insisting on a pre-condition that everybody knows cannot be achieved because it was there for two years and it didn't achieve anything. We should look at the solutions. And there are plenty of solutions that can be

found. And I can share with you a number of solutions that were offered by Iran, and unfortunately there were no takers.

ROBBINS: So Richard, multiple wrongs make a right in this
case, or do you find some empathy for the ambassador's position?

HAASS: In a word, no. I respect him, this ambassador, tremen-
dously. We go back a long ways. But out of all the arguments I've heard
him make over the years, this was the least persuasive. It reminds me
of that saying in courts where if you've got the facts and the evidence
on your side, you argue those, if not, you argue the law. Here Iran
does not have the substance by its side, so it's arguing atmospherics.

You can always find in diplomacy distractions and arguments
for doing or not doing what it is you either want to do or don't want
to do, and that's essentially what we heard. But the Security Council,
regardless of what Mr. Bolton might have said, regardless of what
the United States might want—quite honestly, I wish the Security
Council were a tool of American foreign policy, but it's not. You've
got four other countries with very different points of view. Anyone
doubting that can look at the resolution—the so-called Second
Resolution before the Iraq war. Clearly France and others were not
tools of American foreign policy. And we can look at Russian foreign policy now and Chinese foreign policy on, say, Darfur. The
Security Council is hardly a tool of American foreign policy, and we
can look at Iran. And Russian foreign policy is hardly synonymous
with American foreign policy.

So the Security Council, for better or for worse, is not a tool
of American foreign policy. It's an expression, essentially, of what
the five permanent members agree or disagree on. And in this case,
there's actually significant agreement about what ought to be expected of Iran. That Iran ought not to be in the business of enriching
uranium, ought not to be in the business of doing things outside the
jurisdiction of the International Atomic Energy Agency, ought not to
be going down the path of developing nuclear weapons.

I do not see this as a tool of American foreign policy, I see this
as an expression of international order. And I would hope that Iran
would see fit to agree with it, because I don't believe it is being asked
to do anything that is against Iran's own national interests. And I
think as part of a diplomatic, negotiated package it would benefit

not just the world, but Iran would be better off if it were to reenter compliance and cooperation with the IAEA.

ROBBINS: So there's been a lot of talk recently about the idea of rather than getting caught in more of this "after you suspend" problem that we seem to have, would Iran be willing—can you make that commitment today that if the Security Council would say, okay, as of 12:01 A.M., we'll suspend an effort for sanctions if you will suspend uranium enrichment, so that we can get the talks back moving forward?

ZARIF: You are basically repeating what is already in the Security Council resolution. You're not giving a lot of incentives for Iran. The point is, we can continue to argue what happened in this process until the end of the day. And Richard can point to international legality, and I'm happy to see the United States—and unfortunately, Richard is outside the government—but I'm happy to see the United States sticking so much to international legality. That would be an important development for all of us.

But let's not get involved in that. We know how the Security Council operates. We know how the Security Council was prevented from even passing a cease-fire resolution [in Lebanon], so let's not get into that. We have our own history with the Security Council, the way the Security Council miserably dealt with the Iran/Iraq war. So I don't want to get into things that after ten, twenty years, people will find out how miserably the Security Council acted or reacted to a certain thing.

Let's discuss how we can—I think this conference is about non-proliferation—how we can help nonproliferation. Now, if we start from the assumption and agree on two fundamental starting points, that you do not want to have nuclear weapons proliferated and you do not want to see Iran becoming a nuclear weapon state. And at the same time, you want to respect the inalienable right of Iran to develop nuclear technology for peaceful purposes. If we can agree—and I think these are very simple propositions, but it's very difficult to agree on these two very simple propositions—if we can agree on these two simple propositions and see how best we can achieve them, I believe there are ways much more effective than this so-called panacea of suspension that could in fact achieve these goals.

If the suspension was in fact a resolution, a solution to this issue, why was it that Iran had the suspension for two years, and negotiated, but we did not reach a solution? Because there was no will
to reach a solution. Let us agree on these two fundamental points,
that Iran should never have nuclear weapons—and I would be the
first one to join you in committing my country to this goal that Iran
should never have nuclear weapons. In fact, everybody who has nuclear weapons should abandon them because nuclear weapons no
longer bring security to anybody. And I think if we recognized that,
we would have been—we would go a long way in addressing the
problem.

But that is a goal, that is an objective, and I don't want to talk
about objectives. Let's take the issue at hand. Iran should never have
nuclear weapons. But Iran should have the right to develop nuclear
technology. What are the ways of doing this? How can the international community—and let's not confuse international community
with the Security Council; I can quote for you statements by the
non-aligned 118 members of the international community who are
on record saying that nobody could impose on Iran its choice on fuel
cycle technologies. But let's not even discuss that, because I don't
want to get into basically rhetorical discussions.

Let us say how we can make sure that the international community, if it has concern, could be allayed about Iran's nuclear program—that it will always remain peaceful. And at the same time,
Iran's right would be observed. Because if you ask Iran to abandon
its right, that is not a good recipe for finding a solution and for maintaining nonproliferation.

ROBBINS: Richard, one might say that if Iran hasn't yet crossed
the point of no return, it's pretty close. Because the issue is not really
how much U-236 they produce, or how much they can then enrich,
or what level of enrichment—this is the sort of thing that happens in
people's brains. Unfortunately in Iran, it's only in the brains of men,
and not women, but we won't talk about that today.

ZARIF: Where did you hear that?

ROBBINS: I've been just noticing what your government looks
like. But if they are close to the intellectual point of no return, time

is on their side. We can talk about the legality versus the question of law. We can talk about this. How do we get out of this box? Because time appears to be on Tehran's side, and that's not a good thing.

HAASS: Well I'm not sure time is on Iran's side. Time simply could be on the side of no one, because it could force countries to contemplate actions which could be in no one's interest. So I'm not sure time is on Iran's side or anybody else's.

A lot depends upon what Iran is interested in. If Iran is interested in access to nuclear materials for generating electricity—access to, not physical control of—there's no problem. The Russians and others have made fairly imaginative offers of access to all the nuclear power anyone could want. So if this is an energy issue, there ought not to be a problem.

If the question is not simply that, but what Ambassador Zarif described as Iran's inalienable right to—I don't want to put words in your mouth—but to, what, explore nuclear technology, to enrich uranium, what have you, the question then is, under who's auspices? What controls and assurances does the international community have? Essentially, how is that right defined and limited?

And I'd say one other thing—countries have rights all the time. International relations is not about an Oxford junior common room debate about whether one possesses rights. What international relations is about is the exercise of rights or, at times, the choice of not exercising rights. Indeed, international restraint often depends upon countries deciding *not* to exercise what they may have legal or other rights to do or the capacities to do in the overall—in their own self-interests as well as in the interests in regional and global order.

So coming back, this is all a long-winded way of saying I think there are diplomatic and negotiated outcomes here that are possible, that certainly have not been precluded, have not been meaningfully explored. I would say that before we go down a path implicit in your question where the world has to face one of two choices: either an Iran that accumulates a significant amount of enriched uranium outside IAEA controls, which no one wants to see, which would give them a weapon option in short order; or the use of military force, which would bring into play all sorts of possibilities that again might be in no one's interest. I would think it's in the interest of everybody—not just Iran and the United States, but everybody—to fully explore whether there is a diplomatic or negotiating outcome. And I would simply say I think there is, in principle, one that could be negotiated. And secondly, I don't believe that we have done, no party has done all that they might to demonstrate that it's not there.

I mean diplomacy always has two purposes. One is to reach agreement. The other is also to show that you can't reach agreement. And then if you can't reach agreement, then you can, with an open mind, fully then weigh the alternatives. I don't think we have reached that point in the case of Iran, and I would think it makes sense to reach that point. To essentially fully explore diplomacy— not, by the way, as a stalling tactic, not as a way to allow Iran to continue to simply enrich uranium for as long as it wants—but I think that one should be able to have a diplomacy that at the same time would prevent Iran from going down that path voluntarily, it would unilaterally decide not to exercise what it determines is its right. And then hopefully, as in the case say we've seen in other parts of the world, most recently with North Korea, there is the possibility of at least reaching agreements that might be mutually acceptable.

ROBBINS: So what would it take for your government to agree to re-suspend the enrichment of uranium so that talks could continue?

ZARIF: Well, you see. . . .

ROBBINS: Or under no conditions will you. . . .

ZARIF: Well, you see the issue is to find, as Richard said, a modality or a number of modalities where the international community—or those who are concerned in the international community—could be assured that Iran would never pursue nuclear weapons. Now, I don't agree with a lot of innuendoes in Richard's remarks, but I agree with his conclusion. I do not believe that under the current circumstances, anything that Iran does in the area of enrichment is outside the control of the IAEA. In fact, the IAEA has cameras, is watching what we're doing in that area.

We have offered to do even more. We have offered to allow— when we offered in 2005 to allow the IAEA to have a permanent presence on our sites. Now, that is something that no other country has offered. We offered that. That is beyond the Additional Protocol. But we did offer that. So Iran does not want to do anything outside the view of the IAEA. You can rest assured that we want to make sure that the IAEA looks at what we are doing and is able to monitor what we are doing.

But there are ways of reaching that even to the satisfaction of everybody, if people are ready to look for resolution. If you have a preconceived idea about what a resolution would look like and want to impose that preconceived idea, even before you start the process—a tactic that has already been used and exhausted in my view, without much conclusion—then you're precluding the possibility of looking for alternatives.

I believe what Richard said, talking about modalities that would prevent Iran from making nuclear weapons—in addition to the fact that Iran doesn't want to make nuclear weapons, and I don't draw any parallels between Iranian case and the North Korean case because we have stated very clearly, unlike North Korea, that we do not want to have nuclear weapons. We do not believe that nuclear weapons help our national security. So the way to do it is to find those modalities.

Now, addressing the issue of time being on this side or the other side. Secretary Rice made a statement on the 31st of May where she put an impossible precondition for those negotiations. Now, Richard says that we should not allow Iran to continue to move forward. But the point is we have already lost, what, seven months? No, even more. Almost ten months. Which could have been used for negotiations and Iran was ready to negotiate. We had proposals on the table to be negotiated. People did not even look at those proposals.

I would submit to you that it would be in the interests of everybody to start looking at those proposals. To see whether there is any element that could be used in order to provide these assurances. Now, red lines have always existed. I remember Richard when you were in government, the red line was Bushehr. The red line was not enrichment but actual nuclear power plants. Now that red line has shifted. It can reshift. It can reshift back to Bushehr, as it did during the consultations on the second draft resolution in the Security Council, where the argument was raised that even Bushehr was dangerous.

So we've seen these shifting red lines. Now, let us not talk about arbitrary red lines. We have an international agreement. We have mechanisms. We have the MNA report, the Multilateral Nuclear Approaches to fuel cycle technologies that have been produced by the IAEA. The MNA report provides five alternatives in order to reach a—the guarantee that is necessary that countries are not developing nuclear weapons in the name of developing nuclear fuel. So we can explore those. Iran has been prepared to accept and to implement for the first time—and is the only country that has accepted—three of those five suggestions.

So let us start talking about those and finding a way in order to address the problem rather than insisting on an impossible precondition. Which did not resolve the problem then, and I can tell you that it does not address the security concerns that are being raised by people. That in Iran, the knowledge has been created. However it was created, the knowledge is there.

And to address your question, one of the people who is very knowledgeable in this area is a lady. So it's a discussion that has been done by both genders. It's not a gender-specific discussion. She was tougher than I was in the negotiations in Paris.

ROBBINS: So just to point out, I didn't—I haven't missed the point that you didn't actually answer my question about what it would take for suspension but—because you were answering a much larger, more strategic, and I was asking a tactical question. But since my softball time is almost running out and I want to share it with everybody else, let's go into final jeopardy here and very quickly, just do the very, very short responses but for the biggest of questions.

I'm going to ask both of you, what is your idea of what a deal is that could get us out of the problem we have right now? Just give me the four aspects of it that you feel would address America's concerns—or the concerns of the international community, more to the point. I will make this point here, which is the red line of Bushehr was not a red line for the UN Security Council, it might have been a red line for the Clinton Administration or for the Bush Administration. There's a pretty big difference here about shifting red lines. You've been ordered to do something by the Security Council which is very different from being told that there's a red line by a particular U.S. administration.

But beyond that, let's talk about what the outlines of a deal is. Do you want to go first, Richard, and see what you think would be a deal that might work?

HAASS: Sure. One can imagine a deal that was a nuclear-only deal, or one can imagine a broader deal between the United States and Iran that each side would be permitted if you will, to introduce other aspects of the other's policy that gave them pause. So from the United States' point of view, a comprehensive deal would obviously deal with terrorism issues, Iranian support for Hamas, Hezbollah, questions of its opposition to Israel and the peace process. So one could imagine a comprehensive deal, and the only reason I say that is the more comprehensive a deal and to the extent one got satisfaction on a broader range of problems, the more one could put on the table in return in terms of assurances, guarantees, economic incentives, and so forth. Obviously if it's a nuclear-only deal, what one can put on the table is constrained.

Let me say one other point, and then I will answer your question. Secondly, it's not enough to have not simply assurances but even clear evidence that Iran is not "developing nuclear weapons." What we want to avoid is a situation where Iran could develop nuclear weapons in short order. So as a result, what we need to avoid is a situation where Iran is able to develop—even with the IAEA there, it doesn't matter—large amounts of enriched material. Because that would simply—literally and figuratively—shorten the fuse between that point and weaponization.

So IAEA cooperation and presence per se is not enough, non-weaponization is not enough. What we need to do is essentially come up with a negotiation where Iran either does not exercise what it sees as its right, or exercise it only in the most symbolic, limited way—its right to enrich uranium.

And I would think a basic deal is essentially that: That either no enrichment activity or extremely, extremely, extremely limited with extraordinarily intrusive inspection in exchange for whatever arrangements in Iran internationally for access to nuclear power and in exchange for not simply the elimination of certain sanctions but conceivably economic incentives, a degree of political normalization and diplomatic normalization. Possibly certain security assurances. I can imagine essentially, a fairly rich menu of possibilities. But it's got to satisfy the West and the United States would have to—or the world would have to—be satisfied on the nuclear side.

And let me just say I think this whole question of preconditions and the rest could be finessed. What matters in diplomacy is not where you begin a negotiation, it's where you come out and when you come out. So I think it is not beyond the wit and wisdom of diplomats to devise a negotiating process that would get over this hurdle and very quickly get to the point where we were—the United States, Iran or—really Iran and the—better yet—the international community in the expression of the UN Security Council would be talking about the details of the agreement. I do not think this call for a precondition of stoppage of all enrichment activity ought to be allowed to torpedo diplomacy. This is the sort of thing that can be finessed very easily and very quickly I believe.

ROBBINS: Now let me just ask you one follow-up question very quickly just to be clear here, which is that when the Bush Administration came in on the North Korea issue—if you recall when they began what they said was we're not just going to talk about—it's no longer just a nuclear or a missiles issue, this is a wider issue. This has to do with the deployment of conventional forces along the DMZ. They made it so much wider that it paralyzed things, and many people thought that it was made wide *precisely* to paralyze things.

Could you, if you were in government, in a more reasonable Republican administration, could you recommend a mainly nuclear deal that ends up with Iran limited in its inability to—and some assurance that it cannot enrich uranium or enrich enough that we have to worry about it, but that leaves aside the Hamas and Hezbollah issue? That leaves aside internal politics of Iran? And that in exchange gets in some diplomatic relationship and an end of sanctions. Is resolving the nuclear issue enough? Because the Bush Administration has apparently made the decision that it was enough to resolve it in North Korea at the end of the day to leave all those other things off the table.

HAASS: Well, the short answer to that long question is yes. One could design a negotiation which was, if you will, nuclear only, in exchange for certain types of, say, access again to energy, certain types of economic and diplomatic incentives or benefits. All I was saying is the scale of the incentives would have to be proportionate to the full range of Iranian behavior that was being constrained. And to the extent one moves beyond the nuclear program, I can therefore imagine a more generous package of incentives that would be put on the table. But I don't think we ought to insist that everything be resolved before anything can be resolved. So I do think—while it would be preferable to have a comprehensive agreement vis-à-vis Iran, because by definition that would get at questions such as their support for Hamas and Hezbollah, that would obviously be preferable. But if that can't be reached at this point, then I would go for a more modest agreement that would deal with the nuclear issue and, again, having a more modest set of incentives or benefits for Iran and still leave in place certain sanctions or certain potential incentives that would only be triggered—in the positive sense—if Iran addressed other concerns of the Security Council.

And by the way, it's in Iran's interest, I would think, to do that, because Iran has a full range and—needless to say, I'm not going to speak for the Iranian side—but they obviously have concerns about Western and American policy that go way back. They would like those things introduced. And there might be incentive on their side for broadening negotiations. Sometimes broadening negotiations actually simplifies them because it creates the possibility for tradeoffs.

The reason there was not progress with North Korea, I would say—six years ago—was not because the agreement was potentially broad and comprehensive. There were many other reasons. There was not progress. But again, broadening things in some ways, it may make it more complex, but it also does create the possibility of tradeoffs and deals that aren't there if you keep things narrow. So I wouldn't necessarily take an approach that embraced the issues comprehensively as somehow a device to push away the possibility of accord—possibly just the opposite.

ROBBINS: So you only have another month at your job, so let's make a deal before you go.

ROBBINS: Tell us if you. . . .

ZARIF: Richard and I could do that.

ROBBINS: Right, that would be good.

ZARIF: I think that it is possible—more than possible, it's necessary—to find a formula to deal with the nuclear issue. And I venture to add that the nuclear issue is the easiest issue to be resolved because there are objective ways of doing this.

Now, let me just give you what should look like these objective ways. Political commitments. Now I'm talking about the Iranian side. And I'm not that interested in incentives and carrots and sticks. You might have heard what I've said about carrots and stick and all that. So I'm talking about dealing with the nuclear issue on its own issues, and forget about the other things. Now, Iran has no problem with a general understanding, but I do not see this administration here in Washington being prepared for that. So let's deal with the nuclear one and not get too ambitious.

I believe a combination of these: political commitments on peaceful activity. Second, monitoring mechanisms. Third, technical arrangements on the levels, extent, ceilings, that type of stuff. And fourth, a mechanism for cooperation that is from consortium—possibilities of a consortium—that would be there to be participating in the process and making sure that the process would not get out of hand. A combination of these factors would give the necessary assurances. Now, I would agree with Richard that nothing would be fool-proof. But nothing is fool-proof in this world. You want to get as much guarantee as possible that Iran can enjoy its rights, but at the same time any proliferation concern is addressed.

And I think under these four topics, if we start negotiating with those two assumptions—agreement on those two propositions—I believe that we can find a resolution and I believe that there is enough on the table already to find a resolution on the nuclear issue without even addressing these other issues—side issues. I'm not talking about the more global issues, the Iranian grievances against the U.S. and the U.S. concerns about Iran. I'm not talking about those. I'm talking about economic incentives, political incentives, security incentives—those are all nice, but we need to deal with crux of the matter and that is the nuclear issue. And I believe that can be dealt with and it should be dealt with.

ROBBINS: Thank you. I'll throw it open to questions—we have mikes and if you could identify who you are. And we don't want speeches, we genuinely want questions. And Jeff, do you want to start off?

LAURENTI: Sure. Jeff Laurenti, Century Foundation. It's a parallel question for each of you, because Khatami's government had wanted to try to normalize relations in some way with Washington, but other people in Tehran held the leash tight. And then we ended up with the Bush Administration that when Khatami did try to make overtures didn't want to hear it for a while. Who really holds the power in Tehran politics now over the nuclear decisions and over normalization decisions? To what extent does Ahmadinejad—whom the rest of the world does not want to see or doesn't trust—really have a finger on controlling this policy? Or is it lurking somewhere else?

And then to Richard, inside the administration, earlier on when you were within the government, what was the balance of discussion and debate in terms of how close you're willing to get to the Iranians to talk to them? And was regime change then, and do you think regime change is now a major consideration? Is this administration prepared to consider a larger deal?

ZARIF: I think the fact that the West is not prepared to deal with the issue is pushing it to find the excuses: at this time a certain political faction in Iran is not interested in a deal, the other faction is not interested in the deal, this tendency is working for one thing. I think we need to stop looking at excuses and look at solutions. I believe if there is a serious solution, if there is a serious proposal, that we will—with those two fundamental propositions that I talked about—everybody in Iran would be prepared to listen because in Iran, we have decision-making which is constitutionally-based and everybody plays his part. In that decision-making you cannot exclude people who have been elected by the people of Iran because—unfortunately some people have this tendency, if the electorate doesn't elect the people they like, they find ways of excluding them. Look at what's happening in the Palestinian territory to the way the United States is dealing with Hamas.

Let's us deal with the reality. And the reality is it's the package, not the people who you're trying to send the package to. It's the package that is problematic. Let us look at the package that deals with the fundamental issues, and then I can assure you that if everybody in Iran wants a solution and everybody in Iran wants to avoid a confrontation.

ROBBINS: So Richard, who's running the U.S. government? And are they willing to make a deal? (laughter)

HAASS: Well first of all, it's good that you're sitting down because I'm now going to shock you in two ways. One is the idea that there might not be total consensus within the administration on this is just one possibility. And secondly, Jeff, I'm amused that you've asked me in some ways to speak for this administration. I wasn't sure I spoke for them when I worked for them. (laughter)

The idea that I could speak for them now is—the irony, shall we say, doesn't escape me.

Look, this is an administration that has, when it comes to Iran, various tendencies. It worked with it very pragmatically, and both Ambassador Zarif and I were personally part of it when it came to Afghanistan. At the same time, there were many people in the administration who held out, if you will, for regime change. You're seeing the same tendencies with North Korea. I think you see some of the same tendencies now with Iran, which changed because you've also got not simply the nuclear concern. Not simply concerns about terrorism, Hamas, Hezbollah and Israel, but you've also got concerns about Iraq and that whole set of issues—in a tougher energy environment.

But the secretary of state has made clear her willingness and the administration's willingness to speak with Iran. We still have the matter, if you will, of the one precondition, but that's not an existential point. That is a policy point. So that says to me at least, as an outsider, that there has been some, if not movement, at least there's a clear administration position now, which it is willing to talk to Iran. Which suggests that those who have argued that diplomatic interaction with Iran is undesirable because that works against regime change, it seems to me that those people are not dominating administration policy. That rather, what you're seeing is a policy saying we're prepared to have diplomacy: here's the situation or the precondition we want.

Again, we can argue over that. But I'm not hearing, if you will, existential arguments against diplomatic interaction with Iran. That tells me that, again, this is therefore in the realm of the possible, not in the realm of the impossible.

ROBBINS: Thanks. Is that Bill Potter?

POTTER: Thank you very much. My question is for Ambassador Zarif.

ZARIF: Why am I not surprised? (laughter)

POTTER: I would like you to perhaps expand on the fourth point that you identified in the nuclear sector, which was mechanisms for cooperation. And to explore whether this includes various forms of nuclear supply or nuclear assurances. And in particular, whether you see any role for the Russian proposal about a multinational fuel center as being part of that mechanism for cooperation?

ZARIF: Iran has not closed the door to any possibility. We have said that we are prepared to look into various proposals. A proposal that we put on the table, both here in the General Assembly in September 2005 as well as at the conference on disarmament, in I believe it was April or March of 2006, have been international consortium, border-regional consortium based on the suggestions of the MNA. These are the two proposals that we have put on the table—division of labor, division of tasks all have been stated in one way or another in the proposals that were made by Iran.

Now, fuel assurances, you've got—if you want to look at fuel assurances, you've got to look at the case within the Iranian experience. Iran owns fuel outside Iran. We own shares in fuel production conglomerates. We own 10 percent of Eurodif, but that didn't mean that we got a gram of enriched uranium from them, or even raw uranium from any of those. So that is the problem.

How do you want to deal with Iranian concerns? And I haven't heard anybody being prepared to deal with Iranian concerns. And the way Iran has framed this issue in order to find a mutually acceptable way of addressing the problem while at the same time guaranteeing that it will not go in the direction that neither you nor I want it to go—I believe has to be looked at. And I believe it hasn't been looked at because some people have ideas which are basically the worst of Iranian experience.

I think it is important for people to look at the Iranian experience. I think it's important for people to understand that for the past twenty-seven years, Iran has not been able to get anything in the area of advanced technology through official channels. That has been the case all the time, in every case from—you name it—Iran has been prevented from doing it. And that is why Iran has had to go through the other routes. So don't expect us to simply accept that when our European friends come and tell you: we will guarantee it. How can you guarantee it? Can your guarantee be more than owning the company? We still own it. We still sit on the board of directors. But we cannot get a gram of uranium from it.

So it's easy to simply generalize a situation in a country that has decided to forgo fuel production because, you say, it's a buyer's market. Now, I have difficulties with that issue because ten years from now it may not be a buyer's market. But you've got to look at the Iranian experience under—within the framework of Iranian history and see how you can address this. And I think there are ways of addressing it even within that framework.

ROBBINS: So does that mean that if it's an international consortium or a multinational, does it have to be geographically in Iran?

ZARIF: Our proposal has been that Iran is prepared to use its facilities in Iran in order to implement an idea that the IAEA has put on the table, but there has been no takers, in order to make it a multinational facility.

ROBBINS: But it has to be in Iran?

ZARIF: I'm not negotiating on camera what has to be and what has not to be the case, but that is the Iranian proposal, and Iran has said that it is ready to discuss various proposals under appropriate conditions.

ROBBINS: I'm just trying to get a deal before you leave, that's all. (laughter)

I'm sorry. Next—I'd like a little gender balance here, are there any women with their hands up? Oh well. Okay.

COTTA-RAMUSINO: I'm sorry I'm the wrong gender. Nothing I can do about it. My name is Paolo Cotta-Ramusino from Pugwash, Secretary General of Pugwash. The comparison between Iran and North Korea in a sense is very staggering. North Korea always got out of the NPT. They said they wanted to have nuclear weapons. They made nuclear test. And still, at the end, they got talks. Things went in a positive way and presumably have evolved in the right direction. Iran said they don't want to have nuclear weapons. They said they want to have nuclear fuel. There are suspicions about that, but still there are winds of war which is going around and I think are really worrisome.

So my question is essentially to Richard Haass, I guess. How would you explain these different attitude, and is it due to the fact that any military action against North Korea was impossible for logistic reason, since China has its role and so on? Or since South Korea is so much dependent on the (inaudible) activities that could be possibly launched from North Korea that (inaudible) conceive military action in that case? Or is it more to the fact that—we discussed it before—the general role of Iran in the Middle East. And I think if this is the second case, it's important. You can probably understand the sensibility and diffidence of Iranians, who say, well, we do something, and then after that something else will required of us—namely, we don't want you to support anymore Hezbollah or Hamas. Hamas is a different category of its own, in any case.

So I think that, in fact, this confusion is sort of an obstacle to the solution of the problem. So if you want to cut the deal on nuclear issues, it's one thing. If you want really to involve every other issue, I think then it becomes more complicated.

And the final request would be to—that's to Doctor Zarif—is how much do you really think that this irresponsible declaration about the Holocaust and all this kind of very insensitive approach which has been going on in Tehran has complicated the calculation? And how much do you think that this thing could be by the internal democratic process of Iran put to a stop? Thank you.

HAASS: Well, it's difficult for me to answer your question because I believe the United States and Iran should be talking to each other. And I believe there should not be an inconsistency between talking with North Korea and not talking to Iran. I come from the old school of foreign policy where negotiation and diplomacy are simply options in the diplomatic toolkit. It's not a favor we do for anybody, it's not a sign of weakness. It's simply one of the tools of national security. If you can get an agreement that serves your interests on balance, you take it. If you can't, compare it to your other options, and you do one of those other options. So I have a very pragmatic approach.

I would be willing to have a negotiation with Iran; either a narrow agreement on nuclear or a broad agreement on everything else. I'd be prepared to do multiple negotiations with Iran, bilaterally and multilaterally; multilaterally, for example, to deal with the Iraq situation, bilaterally to deal with the nuclear—or conceivably other bilateral matters. I believe we should do it with them in the same way that I believe we should be doing it with North Korea. I welcome the North Korean agreement. It clearly doesn't solve the problem. It begins to deal with the parts of the problem. And one hopes that not only is this agreement implemented but that subsequent agreements are negotiated with North Korea and then are implemented. I would hope the same would happen with Iran.

How to account for the difference? That's difficult. Whether it's a matter of a different calculus, in the sense of China's particular role in the case of North Korea , the fact that you have a multi-party framework. As you say, certain limitations on you as freedom of maneuver given South Korea and so forth. In the case of Iran it's a different set of calculations. But again, as I say, I think in both cases the United States has moved, as I read it, from what you might call a regime change-based policy which precluded negotiations for the most part in both cases. To now, where the United States is having negotiations with North Korea in the six-party talks and seems ready to have negotiations with Iran so long as certain conditions—or in this case, as long as a condition is met. And if I'm right, that at least in principle could be dealt with in the context of negotiations.

So I think there's been some evolution. So it's always dangerous to be optimistic, but I don't see anything that precludes—potentially— there being a negotiation between Iran and be it the United States or others in some sort of a regional framework. And I would hope to see it come about.

ZARIF: Now, the question that you asked, professor. My question would be didn't we have the same problem before the current president came to office? Are we looking for excuses? This is the problem, I started negotiating when President Khatami was in office, and I was the one negotiating. And unfortunately we had a very, very negative experience where extremely generous packages were put on the table by Iran and they were all but disregarded. That was a problem.

Now, we've said the genocide must be condemned, and that position has been repeated again and again, and I do not believe that that has anything to do with this issue. Genocide must be condemned, it should not be an excuse, it should not be an excuse to commit violations against anybody. Holocaust must be condemned. It should never be repeated against anybody. Against the Jews or against the Palestinians or against any other group. It's unfortunate— we today have a decision of the International Court of Justice on genocide. But again, we need to prevent genocide, and we need to condemn genocide whenever and against whomever it happens.

But that has nothing to do with this case because the nuclear problem started long before the current president came to office, and it was not resolved, in spite of Iran's policy of accommodation and in spite of Iran's offers over the two years we suspended enrichment. So neither suspension nor the other stuff are reasons for our failure. The failure is due to the fact that people were not looking for solutions. And if we address that fundamental problem, we will be able to resolve the issue. And unless we address that and look for excuses not to look at the problem and find solutions for the problem, we'll never resolve the problem.

ROBBINS: Well, Richard, Ambassador, I'd like both of you to go in the back of the room and try to work out a deal for us. And very honored to have both of you, and you both argued your cases very strongly and I do hope that we some sort of a solution soon. Thank you very much.

NOTES

CHAPTER 1

1. Interview with Condoleezza Rice, *CNN Late Edition with Wolf Blitzer,* September 8, 2002, transcript available online at http://transcripts. cnn.com/TRANSCRIPTS/0209/08/le.00.html.

2. Public concern about nuclear weapons had waned with the winding down of the Cold War, but rose sharply after the September 11 attacks. Fully 62 percent of Americans polled in 1987 professed to worry about the chances of nuclear war, a concern shared by just 48 percent of respondents in 1994—but those fearful jumped to 56 percent in 2002 (Pew Research Center, "Two Years Later, the Fear Lingers," 2003, available online at http://people-press.org/reports/display.php3?ReportID=192). In the fall of 1997, Pew found that controlling nuclear proliferation ranked high as a foreign policy concern, but behind protecting American jobs ("America's Place in the World II," October 1997, available online at http://people-press.org/reports/display.php3?ReportID=102). When The Century Foundation commissioned opinion research into Americans' attitudes toward foreign policy and national security in January 2005, respondents' top-ranked priority—from a menu of thirty proposed foreign policy goals—was "keeping nuclear weapons away from countries and groups hostile to the U.S. and our allies," selected by 60 percent. Two years later, the same pollster asked a similar question for the American Security Project, and again found nuclear weapons topping the list. Dismantling the Al Qaeda terrorist network came in close behind in both years, but in a sign of shifting priorities, "bringing American troops home from Iraq," which ranked third in 2005, was eclipsed by "promoting and developing alternative energy sources" in 2007. See *American Attitudes toward National Security, Foreign Policy, and the War on Terror,* 2005, p. 6, available online at http://www.tcf.org/list.asp?type=PB&pubid=526; and *America and the World: Evolving Attitudes on National Security and Foreign Policy,* 2007, p. 14, available online at http://www.americansecurityproject.org/files/America%20and%20the%20World.pdf.

CHAPTER 2

1. Jayantha Dhanapala, in "Weapons Threats and International Security: Rebuilding an Unraveled Consensus," *Transcript*, February 26, 2007, available online at http://www.tcf.org/list.asp?type=EV&pubid=176.

2. Ibid.

3. Kofi Annan, "In Larger Freedom: Decision Time at the UN," *Foreign Affairs*, May/June 2005.

4. Michael Krepon, in "Weapons Threats and International Security: Rebuilding an Unraveled Consensus."

5. Filippo Formica, in "Weapons Threats and International Security: Rebuilding an Unraveled Consensus."

6. Hans Blix, in "Weapons Threats and International Security: Rebuilding an Unraveled Consensus."

7. James Leach, in "Weapons Threats and International Security: Rebuilding an Unraveled Consensus."

8. *Weapons of Terror: Freeing the World of Nuclear, Biological and Chemical Arms* (Stockholm: Weapons of Mass Destruction Commission, 2006), available online at http://www.wmdcommission.org/files/Weapons_of_Terror.pdf.

CHAPTER 3

1. Jayantha Dhanapala was the UN under-secretary-general for disarmament affairs from 1998 to 2003 and is a former ambassador of Sri Lanka to the United States. The views expressed here are his own.

2. Nicholas Stern, *The Economics of Climate Change: The Stern Review* (Cambridge: Cambridge University Press, 2007).

3. *IPCC Fourth Assessment Report: Climate Change 2007* (Geneva: Intergovernmental Panel on Climate Change, 2007).

4. In addition to these eight, the Democratic People's Republic of Korea has conducted a nuclear weapons test and purportedly has assembled a handful of nuclear weapons, but has recently agreed to roll back its weapons development program.

5. Jared Diamond, *Collapse: How Societies Choose to Fail or Succeed* (New York: Viking, 2004).

6. See Jayantha Dhanapala, *Multilateral Diplomacy and the NPT—An Insider's Account* (Geneva: UNIDIR, 2005).

7. While India and Pakistan are not parties to the CTBT, as two of the forty-four countries with significant nuclear programs mentioned in an annex, the CTBT will require their signature and ratification to enter into force.

8. George Perkovich, "'Democratic Bomb': Failed Strategy," Carnegie Endowment for International Peace Policy Brief no. 49, November 2006.

9. Henry A. Kissinger, "Diplomacy and Iran's Nuclear Weapons," *San Diego Union-Tribune*, February 13, 2005.

10. *Legality of the Threat or Use of Nuclear Weapons*, International Court of Justice (ICJ) advisory opinion, July 8, 1996. On the necessity of proportionality in deterrence, see Judgment Paragraphs 37–50.

11. *Report of the Canberra Commission on the Elimination of Nuclear Weapons* (Canberra: Australia Department of Foreign Affairs and Trade, August 1996), available online at http://disarm.igc.org/oldwebpages/icjtext. html.

12. *Weapons of Terror: Freeing the World of Nuclear, Biological and Chemical Arms* (Stockholm: Weapons of Mass Destruction Commission, 2006), available online at http://www.wmdcommission.org/files/ Weapons_of_Terror.pdf.

13. George P. Shultz, William J. Perry, Henry A. Kissinger, and Sam Nunn, "A World Free of Nuclear Weapons," *Wall Street Journal*, January 4, 2007, p. A15.

CHAPTER 4

1. Strobe Talbott, *The Master of the Game: Paul Nitze and the Nuclear Peace* (New York: Alfred A. Knopf, 1988), p. 15.

2. *The National Security Strategy of the United States of America* (Washington: The White House, September 2002), p. 1.

CHAPTER 5

1. The Commission for Conventional Armaments of the United Nations Security Council in 1948 defined WMD to be "atomic explosive weapons, radio-active material weapons, lethal chemical and biological weapons, and any weapons developed in the future which have characteristics comparable in destructive effect to those of the atomic bomb." See

Committee on Advances in Technology and the Prevention of their Application to Next Generation Biowarfare Threats, *Globalization, Biosecurity, and the Future of the Life Sciences* (Washington, D.C.: National Academies Press, 2006), p. 53.

2. I distinguish between strategy and policy along the lines of the British military historian Liddell Hart: strategy is "the art of distributing and applying military means to fulfill the ends of policy." See Sir Basil Henry Liddell Hart, *Strategy*, 2d ed. rev. (London: Faber & Faber, 1967), pp. 319–21.

3. The UN Secretary-General's High-level Panel has implicitly defined "international security" in the following way: "Any event or process that leads to large-scale death or lessening of life chances and undermines States as the basic unit of the international system is a threat to international security." *A More Secure World: Our Shared Responsibility: Report of the Secretary-General's High-level Panel on Threats, Challenges and Change* (Geneva: United Nations, 2004), p. 2.

4. This history is discussed in detail in David Holloway, "Deterrence, Preventive War, and Preemption," in *U.S. Nuclear Weapons Policy: Confronting Today's Threats*, George Bunn and Christopher F. Chyba, eds. (Washington, D.C.: Brookings Institution Press, 2006), pp. 34–74.

5. Ibid., pp. 39–43.

6. The *National Security Strategy of the United States of America* declared that "Our forces will be strong enough to dissuade potential adversaries from pursuing a military build-up in hopes of surpassing, or equaling, the power of the United States." See *National Security Strategy of the United States of America* (The White House, September 17, 2002), p. 15, available online at www.whitehouse.gov/nsc/nss.html. Leaked portions of the *Nuclear Posture Review* (January 8, 2002) described three different ways that an adversary might be dissuaded from pursuing a course of action not desired by the United States. The adversary could be dissuaded from pursuing a capability by a recognition that U.S. strikes could reach into its territory and destroy that capability; an adversary could be dissuaded from attacking the United States by a U.S. demonstration of a robust defense against that mode of attack; and an adversary could be dissuaded from competing militarily with the United States by a U.S. capacity to surge the production of its weapons. See excerpts of the *Nuclear Posture Review* available at http://www.globalsecurity.org/wmd/library/policy/dod/npr.htm.

7. The administration (for example, in the 2002 *National Security Strategy*) chose to call preventive war "preemption," but historically "pre-

emption" has been reserved for those cases where one party believes that war is imminent, so strikes first to lessen the damage done by the would-be aggressor.

8. Much greater detail may be found in *U.S. Nuclear Weapons Policy: Confronting Today's Threats*, pp. 297–323.

9. For a discussion of the puzzle of the mismatch between the number of nuclear-capable states and the number of states that have nuclear weapons, see Jacques E. C. Hymans, *The Psychology of Nuclear Proliferation* (Cambridge: Cambridge University Press, 2006), pp. 2 ff.

10. This discussion draws on Christopher F. Chyba, "Toward Biological Security," *Foreign Affairs* 81, no. 3 (2002): 122–36.

11. Robert Carlson, "The Pace and Proliferation of Biological Technologies," *Biosecurity and Bioterrorism* 1, no. 3 (2003): 1–12. For a thorough review of the increase and global spread of these technologies, see *Globalization, Biosecurity, and the Future of the Life Sciences*.

12. Christopher F. Chyba and Alex L. Greninger, "Biotechnology and Bioterrorism: An Unprecedented World," *Survival* 46, no. 2 (2004): 143–62.

13. See Christopher F. Chyba, "Biotechnology and the Challenge to Arms Control," *Arms Control Today*, October 2006, available online at http://www.armscontrol.org/act/2006_10/BioTechFeature.asp.

14. "Report of the UN Secretary-General: Uniting Against Terrorism: Recommendations for a Global Counter-Terrorism Strategy," April 27, 2006, paras. 52–57.

15. International Council for Science-Africa, "Kampala Compact: The Global Bargain for Biosecurity and Bioscience," October 1, 2005.

16. For a review of the current international nuclear weapons landscape, see Christopher F. Chyba and Karthika Sasikumar, "A World of Risk: The Current Environment for U.S. Nuclear Weapons Policy," in *U.S. Nuclear Weapons Policy: Confronting Today's Threats*, pp. 1–33.

CHAPTER 6

1. For useful analyses see Robert J. Einhorn, "The U.S.-India Civil Nuclear Deal," Statement Before the Senate Foreign Relations Committee (April 26, 2006); George Perkovich, "Faulty Promises: The U.S.-India Nuclear Deal," *Policy Outlook* no. 21, Carnegie Endowment for International Peace, September 2005; William C. Potter, "India and the New look of U.S.

Nonproliferation Policy," *Nonproliferation Review* (July 2005): 343–54; Sharon Squassioni, "U.S. Nuclear Cooperation with India: Issues for Congress," Congressional Research Service Report RL 33016, June 27, 2006; and Ashley Tellis, "Should the U.S. Sell Nuclear Technology to India?" Part II, *YaleGlobal* Online, November 10, 2005, available at http://yaleglobal. yale.edu/display.article?id=6487.

2. See the statement by South African Foreign Minister Alfred Nzo in the General Debate at the 1995 Review and Extension Conference on the Parties to the Treaty on the Non-Proliferation of Nuclear Weapons reproduced in Thomas Markram, *A Decade of Disarmament, Transformation and Progress* (Pretoria, South Africa: SaferAfrica, 2004), pp. 137–42. The only component of the package not highlighted in this speech relates to the Middle East, an issue that was promoted forcefully by several states, including Egypt.

3. For an insightful analysis of the 1995 NPT Review and Extension Conference see Jayantha Dhanapala (with Randy Rydell), *Multilateral Diplomacy and the NPT: An Insider's Account* (Geneva: United Nations Institute for Disarmament Research, 2005).

4. The entire list of members is: Australia, Cook Islands, Fiji, Kiribati, Nauru, New Zealand, Niue, Papua New Guinea, Samoa, Solomon Islands, Tonga, Tuvalu, and Vanuatu.

5. See, for example, Harald Müller, "A Treaty in Troubled Waters: Reflections on the Failed NPT Review Conference," *The International Spectator* 40, no. 3 (July–September 2005): 33–44 (especially pp. 43-44); Bruno Tertrais, "The European Union and Nuclear Nonproliferation: Does Soft Power Work?," *The International Spectator* 40, no. 3 (July–September 2005): 45–57; and Oliver Meier, "The European Union's Nonproliferation Strategy: An Interview with Annalisa Giannella, the Personal Representative on Nonproliferation of Weapons of Mass Destruction to EU High Representative Javier Solana," Arms Control Association, July 26, 2005, available online at http://www.armscontrol.org/interviews/ 20050726_Giannella.asp.

6. See the Council of the European Union Web site: http://ue.eu.int/cms3_fo/ showPage.asp?id=392 cited in Tertrais, "The European Union and Nuclear Nonproliferation," p. 48. This common position was adopted in 2004.

7. See Meier, "The European Union's Nonproliferation Strategy."

8. Tertrais, "The European Union and Nuclear Nonproliferation," p. 57.

9. Ibid, p. 56.

10. "EU Aide Worried by Calls to Drop India WMD Clause," Reuters, March 2, 2007, available online at http://www.bilaterals.org/aricle.php3?id_article=7311.

11. See "EU OKs India Joining ITER Nuclear Reactor Project," Reuters, December 2, 2005.

12. Norway and Sweden are conflicted on the issue but appear unwilling to block consensus.

13. Recently, several other NAM members, including Egypt, have expressed frustration that the U.S.-India nuclear deal has complicated efforts to mount pressure against Israeli nuclear activities.

CHAPTER 7

1. George P. Shultz, William J. Perry, Henry A. Kissinger and Sam Nunn, "A World Free of Nuclear Weapons," *Wall Street Journal,* January 4, 2007, p. A15.

CHAPTER 8

1. Statement by UN secretary-general Kofi Annan, 2005 NPT Review Conference, New York, May 2, 2005, available online at http://www.un.org/apps/sg/sgstats.asp?nid=1427.

2. The United States and IAEA are pushing such a scheme under two separate initiatives. See "Nuclear Threat Initiative Commits $50 Million to Create IAEA Nuclear Fuel Bank," Joint NTI/IAEA Press Release 2006/16, September 19, 2006, available online at http://www.iaea.org/NewsCenter/PressReleases/2006/prn200616.html, and "The Global Nuclear Energy Partnership: Greater Energy Security in a Cleaner, Safer World," U.S. Department of Energy, March 2007, available online at http://www.gnep.energy.gov/gnepProgram.html.

3. See e.g., Debra K. Decker and Erwann O. Michel-Kerjan, "A New Energy Paradigm: Ensuring Nuclear Fuel Supply and Nonproliferation through International Collaboration with Insurance and Financial Markets," Belfer Center for Science and International Security, March 2007, pp. 21–22. On the self-defeating character of the U.S. GNEP program's plea to divide the world into fuel supplying nations and fuel recipients, see Edwin Lyman, "The Global Nuclear Energy Partnership: Will It Advance Nonpro-

liferation or Undermine It?" presented at the annual meeting of the Institute of Nuclear Materials Management, July 19, 2006, available at http://www.npec-web.org/Essays/20060700-Lyman-GNEP.pdf and Steve Fetter and Frank N. von Hippel, "Is U.S. Reprocessing Worth the Risk?" *Arms Control Today*, September 2005, available online at http://www.armscontrol.org/act/2005_09/Fetter-VonHippel.asp.

4. "Mexican Working Paper Submitted to the Eighteen Nation Disarmament Committee: Suggested Additions to Draft Nonproliferation Treaty," ENDC/196, September 19, 1967, in U.S. Arms Control and Disarmament Agency, *Documents on Disarmament, 1967*, Publication No. 46 (Washington, D.C.: U.S. Government Printing Office, July 1968), pp. 394–95; "Romanian Working Paper Submitted to the Eighteen Nation Disarmament Committee: Amendments and Additions to the Draft Nonproliferation Treaty," ENDC/199, October 19, 1967, in *ibid.*, pp. 525–526; "Brazilian Amendments to the Draft Nonproliferation Treaty," ENDC/201, October 31, 1967, in U.S. Arms Control and Disarmament Agency, *Documents on Disarmament, 1967*, p. 546; and "Spanish Memorandum to the Co-Chairman of the ENDC," ENDC/210, February 8, 1968, in U.S. Arms Control and Disarmament Agency, *Documents on Disarmament, 1968*, Publication No. 52 (Washington, D.C.: U.S. Government Printing Office, September 1969), pp. 39–40.

5. "Statement by the Swedish Representative [Alva Myrdal] to the Eighteen Nation Disarmament Committee: Nonproliferation of Nuclear Weapons," ENDC/PV. 243, February 24, 1966, in U.S. Arms Control and Disarmament Agency, *Documents on Disarmament, 1966*, Publication No. 43 (Washington, D.C.: U.S. Government Printing Office, September 1967), p. 56.

6. Eldon V. C. Greenberg, "NPT and Plutonium: Application of NPT Prohibitions to 'Civilian' Nuclear Equipment, Technology and Materials Associated with Reprocessing and Plutonium Use," Nuclear Control Institute, 1984 (Revised May 1993).

7. See Report of Main Committee III, Treaty on the Nonproliferation of Nuclear Weapons Review and Extension Conference, May 5, 1995, NPT/CONF.1995/MC.III/1, Sec. I, para. 2 (emphases added) available online at http://www.un.org/Depts/ddar/nptconf/162.htm, which states: "wThe Conference records that the potential benefits of the peaceful applications of nuclear explosions envisaged in article V of the Treaty have not materialized. In this context, the Conference notes that the potential benefits of the peaceful applications of nuclear explosions have not been demonstrat-

ed and that serious concerns have been expressed as to the environmental consequences that could result from the release of radioactivity from such applications and on the risk of possible proliferation of nuclear weapons. Furthermore, no requests for services related to the peaceful applications of nuclear explosions have been received by IAEA since the Treaty entered into force. The Conference further notes that no State party has an active programme for the peaceful application of nuclear explosions."

8. Eldon V. C. Greenberg, "NPT and Plutonium"; Henry D. Sokolski and George Perkovich, "It's Called Nonproliferation," *Wall Street Journal*, April 29, 2005, p. A16.

9. NPT, Art. III, para. 1.

10. For example, see "British Paper Submitted to the Eighteen Nation Disarmament Committee: Technical Possibility of International Control of Fissile Material Production," ENDC/60, August 31, 1962 (Corr. 1, November 27, 1962), in U.S. Arms Control and Disarmament Agency, *Documents on Disarmament, 1962*, Publication No. 19, Vol. 2 of 2 (Washington, D.C.: U.S. Government Printing Office, November 1963), pp. 834–52.

11. See Bayan Rahman, "Japan 'Loses' 206 kg of Plutonium," *Financial Times*, January 28, 2003, available online at http://news.ft.com;servlet/ContentServer?pagename=FT.com/StoryFT/FullStory&c=StoryFT&cid=1042491288304&p=10112571727095, and Nuclear Control Institute, "Enormous 'Plutonium Gap' at Japan's Tokai Plant Highlights Proliferation Risks of Reprocessing," January 28, 2003, available online at http://www.nci.org/03NCI/01/pr12803.htm.

12. In addition to the material unaccounted for at the Japanese plants noted above, the commercial British reprocessing plant at Sellafield reported as missing 19 and 27 kilograms of separated plutonium in 2004 and 2005. See Edwin S. Lyman, "Can Nuclear Fuel Production in Iran and Elsewhere Be Safeguarded Against Diversion?" an essay presented at "After Iran: Safeguarding Peaceful Nuclear Energy," NPEC/King's College-London Conference, London, U.K., October 2005, pp. 10–12, available online at http://www.npec-web.org/Frameset.asp?PageType=Single&PDFFile=Paper050928LymanFuelSafeguardDiv&PDFFolder=Essays.

13. In the case of at least one U.S. HEU fuel fabrication plant operating during the 1960s in Apollo, Pennsylvania, the U.S. Atomic Energy Commission reported that the amount of material unaccounted for was approximately 100 kilograms. Several former senior U.S. officials suspect this material was diverted to Israel's nuclear weapons program. See Seymour M. Hersh, *The Samson Option* (New York: Vintage, 1993), pp. 241–57.

14. On these points, see John Carlson, "Addressing Proliferation Challenges from the Spread of Uranium Enrichment Capability," paper for the annual meeting of the Institute for Nuclear Materials Management, Tucson, July 8–12, 2007; Paul Leventhal, "Safeguards Shortcomings: A Critique," NCI, Washington, D.C., September 12, 1994; Marvin Miller, "Are IAEA Safeguards in Plutonium Bulk-Handling Facilities Effective?" NCI, Washington, D.C., August 1990; Brian G. Chow and Kenneth A. Solomon, *Limiting the Spread of Weapons-Usable Fissile Materials* (Santa Monica, Calif.: RAND, 1993), pp. 1–4; and Marvin Miller, "The Gas Centrifuge and Nuclear Proliferation," in Victor Gilinsky et al., *A Fresh Examination of the Proliferation Dangers of Light Water Reactors* (Washington, D.C.: The Nonproliferation Policy Education Center, October 22, 2004), p. 38, available online at http://www.npec-web.org/Frameset.asp?PageType=Single& PDFFile=20041022-GilinskyEtAl-LWR&PDFFolder=Essays.

15. Victor Gilinsky et al., *A Fresh Examination of the Proliferation Dangers of Light Water Reactors.*

16. See Christopher Ford, "NPT Article IV: Peaceful Uses of Nuclear Energy," statement of the principal deputy assistant secretary of state for verification, compliance and implementation to the 2005 Review Conference of the Treaty on the Non-Proliferation of Nuclear Weapons, New York, May 18, 2005, available online at http://www.state.gov/t/vci/rls/rm/46604.htm.

17. French Republic, "Strengthening the Nuclear Non-Proliferation Regime," working paper submitted to the Preparatory Committee for the 2005 Review Conference of the Parties of the Treaty on the Non-Proliferation of Nuclear Weapons, May 4, 2004, available online at http://disarmament2.un.org/ wmd/npt/2005/PC3-listofdocs.html.

18. See, e.g., Under Secretary of State for Arms Control and International Security John R. Bolton, "Iran's Continuing Pursuit of Weapons of Mass Destruction," testimony before the House International Relations Committee, Subcommittee on the Middle East and Central Asia, June 24, 2004.

19. See, e.g., George W. Bush, "President's Statement on Non-Proliferation of Nuclear Weapons Treaty," White House, Office of the Press Secretary, March 7, 2005, available online at http://www.whitehouse. gov/news/releases/2005/03/20050307-10.html.

20. See "Assessing 'Rights' Under the Nuclear Nonproliferation Treaty," U.S. Congress, House Subcommittee on Terrorism, Nonproliferation, and Human Rights, hearing transcript, March 2, 2006, p. 16 ff., available online at http://commdocs.house.gov/committees/intlrel/ hfa26333.000/hfa26333_0f.htm.

21. Preliminary recognition of these points was most recently made in a Council on Foreign Relations special report on nuclear power. See Charles D. Ferguson, *Nuclear Energy: Balancing Benefits and Risks* (New York: Council on Foreign Relations, April 2007).

22. For more on the current membership and investment and trade principles of the Energy Charter Treaty go to http://www.encharter.org/. The second principle of the Global Energy Charter for Sustainable Development calls for "The establishment of guidelines and internationally standardized methods of evaluation for determining the external effects and total lifecycle costs and risks for all energy systems, taking into account the environmental, health and other damage caused by energy-related activities." See *The Global Energy Charter for Sustainable Development,* available online at http://www.cmdc.net/echarter.html.

23. See "The Energy Challenge: Energy Review Report 2006," British Department of Trade and Industry, July 11, 2006, available online at http://www.dti.gov.uk/energy/review/. The British estimate of the breakeven point for nuclear power's competitiveness with a CO_2 tax of roughly $46 a ton is consistent with earlier U.S. estimates of between $25 and $50 per ton of CO_2 made in a study by the Massachusetts Institute of Technology. See *The Future of Nuclear Power* (Cambridge, Mass.: Massachusetts Institute of Technology, 2003), pp. 41–43.

24. See "EC Will Investigate 'Green Power' Complaint of State Aid to TVO EPR," *Nucleonics Week,* January 13, 2005. According to the complaint, the project is enjoying subsidized loans and French export loan credits and the final decision to buy the plant was made on the basis of an unsound study rather than competitive bidding.

25. For an historical and legal analysis of the NPT, see Robert Zarate, "The NPT, IAEA Safeguards and Peaceful Nuclear Energy: An Inalienable Right But Precisely to What?" a draft paper presented at an NPEC/FRS Conference, "Assessing the Ability of the IAEA to Safeguard Peaceful Nuclear Energy," Paris, France, November 11–12, 2006, available online at http://www.npec-web.org/Essays/20070301-Zarate-NPT-IAEA-Peaceful-Nuclear.pdf.

26. See David Sanger and William Broad, "With Eye on Iran, Rivals Also Want Nuclear Power," *New York Times,* April 15, 2007, and Henry Sokolski, "Hair Raising New World," *Wall Street Journal,* December 15, 2006.

CHAPTER 9

1. George P. Shultz, William J. Perry, Henry A. Kissinger, and Sam Nunn, "A World Free of Nuclear Weapons," *Wall Street Journal*, January 4, 2007, p. A15.

2. Statement by Stephen G. Rademaker, "U.S. Compliance with Article VI of the Non-Proliferation Treaty (NPT)," U.S. Department of State, February 3, 2005, available online at http://www.state.gov/t/ac/rls/rm/41786.htm.

3. "Report of the Canberra Commission on the Elimination of Nuclear Weapons," January 30, 1997, available online at http://www.dfat.gov.au/cc/cchome.html

4. Matthew Bunn, "Anecdotes of Insecurity," Nuclear Threat Initiative, last updated on January 16, 2004, available online at http://www.nti.org/e_research/cnwm/threat/anecdote.asp. The Center for Nonproliferation Studies at the Monterey Institute for International Studies maintains a more comprehensive public database, NIS Nuclear Trafficking Database, Center for Nonproliferation Studies, last updated June 30, 2006, available online at http://www.nti.org/db/nistraff/index.html.

5. Matthew Bunn and Anthony Weir, *Securing the Bomb, 2006* (Cambridge, Mass., and Washington, D.C.: Project on Managing the Atom, Harvard University, and Nuclear Threat Initiative, July 2006). Figures are from unpublished data provided by Department of Energy, May 2006.

6. Brian D. Finlay and Andrew J. Grotto, "The Race to Secure Russia's Loose Nukes," Center for American Progress, September 13, 2005, available online at http://www.americanprogress.org/atf/cf/%7BE9245FE4-9A2B-43C7-A521-5D6FF2E06E03%7D/NUKES.PDF.

7. See recommendations from: John P. Holdren, "The Threat from Surplus Nuclear-Bomb Materials," testimony to the U.S. Senate Foreign Relations Committee, Subcommittee on Europe, 104th Congress, 1st Session, August 23, 1995; *Combating Proliferation of Weapons of Mass Destruction: Report from the Commission to Assess the Organization of the Federal Government to Combat the Proliferation of Weapons of Mass Destruction* (Washington, D.C.: Deutch Commission, July 1999), available online at http://www.fas.org/spp/starwars/program/deutch/11910book.pdf); and *A Report Card on the Department of Energy's Nonproliferation Programs with Russia* (Washington, D.C.: U.S. Department of Energy, Secretary of Energy Advisory Board, January 10, 2001), available online at http://www.seab.energy.gov/publications/rpt.pdf.

8. Graham Allison, *Nuclear Terrorism: The Ultimate Preventable Catastrophe* (New York: Times Books, 2004).

9. Amy F. Woolf, "Nonproliferation and Threat Reduction Assistance: U.S. Programs in the Former Soviet Union," CRS Report for Congress, updated June 26, 2006, available online at http://www.fas.org/sgp/crs/nuke/RL31957.pdf. The total includes $415.5 million for the Cooperative Threat Reduction (CTR) Program at the Department of Defense, $530 million for nonproliferation programs at the Department of Energy, and $71 million for programs at the State Department.

10. Anthony Wier, William Hoehn, and Matthew Bunn, "Threat Reduction Funding in the Bush Administration," Managing the Atom Project, Harvard University, and Russian-American Nuclear Security Advisory Council, October 6, 2004, available online at http://bcsia.ksg.harvard.edu/BCSIA_content/documents/funding_debate_100604.pdf.

11. For proposals favoring an increase in CTR funding, see Lawrence J. Korb and Robert O. Boorstin, "Integrated Power: A National Security Strategy for the 21st Century," The Center for American Progress, June 7, 2005, p. 33, available online at http://www.americanprogress.org/site/pp.asp?c=biJRJ8OVF&b=742277. Total threat-reduction spending: Woolf, "Nonproliferation and Threat Reduction Assistance." Missile defense request: "Missile Defense Budget Request for FY 2007," Center for Defense Information, February 8, 2006, available online at http://www.cdi.org/friendlyversion/printversion.cfm?documentID=3301. Total nuclear spending: "about $11 billion a year will go to operating, maintaining and modernizing the bombers, submarines, and missiles that carry the 6,000 operational nuclear weapons in the American arsenal, with the remaining $6 billion going towards maintaining the warheads. During the Cold War, the United States spent less than $4 billion a year on average on these nuclear weapons activities." Miriam Pemberton and Lawrence Korb, "Report of the Task Force on a Unified Security Budget for the United States, 2007," International Relations Center, May 3, 2006, available online at http://www.fpif.org/fpiftxt/3253.

12. Allison, *Nuclear Terrorism*, p. 78.

13. U.S. Department of Defense, Nuclear Posture Review Report, January 8, 2002, available online at http://www.globalsecurity.org/wmd/library/policy/dod/npr.htm. Christopher Paine, "Weaponeers of Waste," Natural Resources Defense Council, April 2004, available online at http://www.nrdc.org/nuclear/weaponeers/weaponeers.pdf. "Our Hidden WMD Program: Why Bush Is Spending So Much on Nuclear Weapons,"

Slate, April 23, 2004, available online at http://www.slate.com/id/2099425/.

14. The 2000 Review Conference Final Document included thirteen practical steps for systematic implementation of Article VI of the NPT, and of Paragraphs 3 and 4(c) of the 1995 Decision on "Principles and Objectives for Nuclear Non-Proliferation and Disarmament." See The United Nations, "Final Document 2000 Review Conference of the Parties to the Treaty of the Non-Proliferation of Nuclear Weapons," May 2000, available online at http://disarmament.un.org/wmd/npt/finaldoc.html.

15. Assistant Secretary of State for Arms Control Stephen Rademaker argues this point in his statement at the 2005 NPT Review Conference, UN General Assembly, May 2, 2005: "The United States remains fully committed to fulfilling our obligations under Article VI. Since the last review conference the United States and the Russian Federation concluded our implementation of START I reductions, and signed and brought into force the Moscow Treaty of 2002" (available online at http://www.un.int/usa/05_089.htm).

16. National Research Council of the National Academies, *Effects of Nuclear Earth-Penetrator and Other Weapons* (Washington, D.C.: National Academies Press, 2005), executive summary available online at http://newton.nap.edu/execsumm_pdf/11282.

17. Robert W. Nelson, for example, makes some of these points in "Nuclear Bunker Busters, Mininukes, and the U.S. Nuclear Stockpile," *Physics Today* 56, no. 11 (2003): 32–37.

18. Pemberton and Korb, "Report of the Task Force on a Unified Security Budget."

19. Rademaker statement, 2005 NPT Review Conference.

20. Ibid.

21. Ashton B. Carter and Stephen A. LaMontagne, "A Fuel-Cycle Fix," *The Bulletin of the Atomic Scientists* (January/February 2006): 24–25, available online at http://bcsia.ksg.harvard.edu/publication.cfm?program=CORE&ctype=article&item_id=1345.

22. Such a program must be structured in such a way that it does not accentuate the problem by subsidizing the expansion of nuclear plants in countries where they would otherwise not be economically feasible. This danger is discussed by Henry Sokolski, "Market-Based Nonproliferation," testimony presented before a Hearing of the House Committee on Foreign Affairs, May 10, 2007, available online at http://www.npec-web.org/Testimonies/20070510-Sokolski-HCFA-PreparedTestimony.pdf.

23. "IAEA Chief Promotes Nuclear Fuel Plan," Nuclear Threat Initiative, October 6, 2005, available online at http://www.nti.org/d_newswire/issues/2005/10/6/6C312C3F-16BC-4720-9AD8-74016A16AE1D.html.

24. Michael O'Hanlon and Mike M. Mochizuki, *Crisis on the Korean Peninsula: How to Deal With a Nuclear North Korea* (New York: McGraw-Hill, 2003), pp. 16–21.

25. In August 2006, reporter Steve Coll wrote "I gather that in private briefings the Bush Administration's intelligence analysts focus on a five-to-seven-year window." Steve Coll, "Blueprints for Disaster," *New Yorker,* August 2006, available online at http://www.newyorker.com/online/content/articles/060807on_onlineonly.

26. See Bruce Jentleson, "Sanctions against Iran: Key Issues," The Century Foundation, February 1, 2007, and Flynt L. Leverett, "Dealing with Tehran: Assessing U.S. Diplomatic Options toward Iran," The Century Foundation, December 4, 2006.

27. *A Report Card on the Department of Energy's Nonproliferation Programs with Russia.*

28. For one example, see "Statement on Nuclear Weapons by International Generals and Admirals," Proposition One, December 5, 1996, available online at http://prop1.org/2000/genint.htm.

29. See, for example, the Associated Press/Ipsos Poll, conducted by Ipsos-Public Affairs, March 21–23, 2005, which found 66 percent of American respondents agreeing that "No countries should be allowed to have nuclear weapons" versus 13 percent that said "Only the United States and its allies should be allowed to have nuclear weapons," available online at http://www.pollingreport.com/defense.htm.

INDEX

About the Contributors

Hans Blix is chairman of the Weapons of Mass Destruction Commission. He served in the Swedish foreign ministry from 1963 to 1976, and in 1978 became Sweden's minister for foreign affairs. He served as director general of the International Atomic Energy Agency from 1981 until 1997. He was appointed in 2000 to his present position as head of the United Nations Monitoring, Verification, and Inspection Commission (UNMOVIC). He has written several books on subjects associated with international and constitutional law.

Christopher F. Chyba is professor of astrophysical sciences and international affairs at the Woodrow Wilson School, Princeton University. Previously, he was codirector of the Center for International Security and Cooperation (CISAC), where he also directs the Program on Science and Global Security at Stanford University. In October 2001, he was named a MacArthur Fellow for his work in planetary science and international security. He served on the White House national security staff from 1993 to 1995. His most recent book is *U.S. Nuclear Weapons Policy: Confronting Today's Threats* (Brookings, 2006), which he coedited with George Bunn.

Joseph Cirincione is a senior fellow and director for nuclear policy at the Center for American Progress. Prior to joining the Center in May 2006, he served as director for nonproliferation at the Carnegie Endowment for International Peace for eight years. He worked for nine years in the U.S. House of Representatives on the professional staff of the Committee on Armed Services and the Committee on Government Operations, and served as staff director of the Military Reform Caucus. He is the author of *Bomb Scare: The History and Future of Nuclear Weapons* (Columbia University Press, 2007) as well as over two hundred articles on defense issues, a frequent commentator in the media, and has given over one hundred talks around the world in the past two years.

JAYANTHA DHANAPALA was UN under-secretary-general for disarmament affairs from 1998 to 2003 and the president of the 1995 NPT Review and Extension Conference. Joining the Sri Lanka Foreign Service in 1965, he served in London, Beijing, Washington, D.C., and New Delhi before being appointed ambassador to the United Nations in Geneva and ambassador to the United States. He was also additional foreign secretary and, on a leave of absence from 1987 to 1992, he was director of the United Nations Institute for Disarmament Research (UNIDIR). He has also served as commissioner in UNSCOM, the head of the Special Group visiting the Presidential Sites in Iraq, and a member of the 1996 Canberra Commission on the Elimination of Nuclear Weapons. He has published four books and several articles, is the recipient of four honorary doctorates and several international awards, and was a candidate for secretary-general of the United Nations. He is a member of the Weapons of Mass Destruction Commission, the Governing Board of SIPRI, and the chairman of the UN University Council.

MICHAEL KREPON is the cofounder of the Henry L. Stimson Center. He has worked previously in the Carter Administration, on Capitol Hill, and at the Carnegie Endowment for International Peace. His most recent books are *Cooperative Threat Reduction, Missile Defense, and the Nuclear Future* (Palgrave, 2005); *Space Assurance or Space Dominance? The Case Against Weaponizing Space* (Henry L. Stimson Center, 2003); *Nuclear Risk Reduction in South Asia* (editor; Palgrave, 2004); and *Escalation Control and the Nuclear Option in South Asia* (coeditor; Henry L. Stimson Center, 2004). He is a diplomat scholar at the University of Virginia, where he teaches in the Politics Department.

JEFFREY LAURENTI is senior fellow at The Century Foundation, where he directs the foundation's foreign policy work. Previously, as a senior adviser to the United Nations Foundation, he served as deputy director of the United Nations and Global Security initiative. He was executive director of policy studies at the United Nations Association of the United States until 2003, currently serves on the association's board of directors, and also is a member of the Council on Foreign Relations. He was a candidate for the U.S. House of Representatives in 1986, senior issues adviser to the Mondale/Ferraro campaign in 1984, and from 1978 to 1984 was executive director of the New Jersey Senate. He is the author of monographs on the subjects of international peace and security, terrorism, UN reform, and international narcotics policy.

WILLIAM C. POTTER is Institute Professor and director of the Center for Nonproliferation Studies at the Monterey Institute of International Studies (MIIS). He has served as a consultant to the Arms Control and Disarmament Agency, Lawrence Livermore National Laboratory, the RAND Corporation, and the Jet Propulsion Laboratory. His present research focuses on nuclear terrorism and on proliferation issues involving the post-Soviet states. He is a member of the Council on Foreign Relations, the Pacific Council on International Policy, and the International Institute for Strategic Studies, and served for five years on the UN secretary-general's Advisory Board on Disarmament Matters and the board of trustees of the UN Institute for Disarmament Research. He was an adviser to the delegation of Kyrgyzstan to the 1995 NPT Review and Extension Conference and to the 1997, 1998, 1999, 2002, 2003 and 2004 sessions of the NPT Preparatory Committee, as well as to the 2000 and 2005 NPT Review Conferences. He is, most recently, coauthor of *The Four Faces of Nuclear Terrorism* (Routledge, 2005).

CARL ROBICHAUD is a program officer at The Century Foundation, where he writes on nonproliferation and counterterrorism policy and directs the foundation's Afghanistan Watch program. Prior to that, he was a program officer with the Global Security Institute where he worked on issues of arms control and disarmament. He was selected in 2003 as a Harold W. Rosenthal Fellow for international affairs and security. His media appearances include CNN and the BBC, and his writing has appeared in numerous online and print publications.

HENRY D. SOKOLSKI is the executive director of the Nonproliferation Policy Education Center, a Washington-based nonprofit organization he founded in 1994. He has been a resident fellow at the National Institute for Public Policy, the Heritage Foundation, and the Hoover Institution. He served from 1989 to 1993 as deputy for nonproliferation policy in the Office of the Secretary of Defense, where he received the Secretary's Medal for Outstanding Public Service, and before that in the Office of Net Assessment on proliferation issues. He currently serves as an adjunct professor at the Institute of World Politics in Washington and has taught courses at the University of Chicago, Rosary College, and Loyola University. He is the author or editor of a number of works on proliferation related issues, including *Gauging U.S.–Indian Strategic Cooperation* (Strategic Studies Institute, 2007) and *Best of Intentions: America's Campaign against Strategic Weapons Proliferation* (Praeger, 2001).